MW01698183

6

Choir Director
BASICS

Oliver Douberly

PASTORAL PRESS
PORTLAND • OREGON

ISBN: 1-56929-043-1

Pastoral Press
A division of OCP Publications
5536 NE Hassalo
Portland, OR 97213
Phone 1-800-LITURGY (548-8749)
E-mail: liturgy@ocp.org
Website: www.ocp.org

Printed in the United States of America

Contents

Preface

This book is about music making and the craft of music as it relates to church choirs and the people who serve their parishes through the ministry of music. It is intended to be a practical, down-to-earth companion, diary, and guide to help us be more effective in that ministry. It is not intended to be the last word in matters choral, but to provide us a practical starting place for thinking through important musical matters. Most of the information presented here is drawn from a personal experience of twenty-five years of working with choir directors and choirs of all kinds. In many cases I am simply the messenger, handing on timeless techniques and ideas that have been passed on to me from many colleagues and my beloved teachers: Mildred Andrews Boggess, Professor of Organ and Dr. Bev Henson, Professor of Choral Music at the University of Oklahoma during my study years there.

I would like to thank Margie Feighny for helping with the initial manuscript and Donna Robillard for proof reading the work. I especially would like to thank Dr. Glenn Byer for his tireless efforts and creative editing ideas in the process, and finally, to Darwin Bragg, without whose constant love and support, none of this would have come to fruition. Finally I must thank the hundreds and hundreds of choir directors of the Catholic Church who have shared their insights and allowed me a view of the enormous potential of music as art and prayer.

My only goal is to share my experiences with you, the reader; what you do with the material has to be your decision. If you find one thing useful, I will have accomplished my task. God bless us all.

Oliver Douberly

Why Sing in the Choir

Prologue

What makes singing in the choir so special anyway? Almost anyone, with even the smallest amount of motivation, can join their church choir. In today's church, choirs come in such a variety of sizes and shapes that there is literally a choir for everyone! Regardless of your taste or preference in music, your musical training, even your vocal gifts, there is a spot for you, as a singer, in a local church choir. It is one of the few remaining places in our world where the person who loves to sing (with the radio, in the shower, anywhere) can share that love in a public way.

Once you have begun and have taken your place among the other sisters and brothers in the choir, you realize that you are among people who share to a greater or lesser extent your love for music, commitment to music in liturgy, and deep faith in the power of the ritual celebrations in the faith life of the church. There exists a true community among those of us who share our talents in the wonderful world of singing our faith. Through NPM Choir Director Institutes and my clinician work with Oregon Catholic Press, I have enjoyed the luxury of meeting and sharing experiences with choir directors from all over the United States. I have had the happy privilege of hearing the choirs of the Catholic Church across America through the ears of the ministers of music who bring them together. The sound painting that is created by these choirs has every color of the rainbow. Listening to that painting has allowed me to ponder more deeply what it means to think of the "ministry of the choir." It is definitely a two-sided coin.

The first side concerns music. All music is discipline. Choral music, like ensemble music of any kind, is particularly dependent on discipline. The discipline of the music itself, as given to us by the composer/editor/arranger, brings a thousand details to bear on every note we sing. We are asked not only to sing every note in tune, and in correct volume and length, but we must do it with perfect diction of the text and in perfect balance with the rest of the choir. What a tall order! Every singer is responsible for his or her own discipline, and the choir director is responsible for drawing all disciplines together and providing the director's discipline on top of them all! We all know that it is only after this discipline is second nature that we begin to actually make the music. How can all of this discipline walk hand in hand with ministry? I know it can, and it must.

The second side is the area of ministry. Ministry is service. When we are in service to a kaleidoscope of people, ministry becomes, of necessity, a rather messy proposition. How we minister to one person is different from ministering to another. When music is ministry, the musical preferences and tastes and the music that sings to the faith life of the people we serve have to be taken into account. It is not easy to draw a plan for such a ministry. It is messy. It is not possible to apply principles of discipline in ministry in the same way as one can in music.

How does one relate discipline with service and begin to define the ministry of the choir? We already know the answer to this question, but perhaps we have not developed the vocabulary to speak easily to one another about it. The purpose of this book is to help develop that way of speaking, to establish a basic structure for a choir which takes account of both these truths. As a book of basics, a few definitions are in order before we proceed to these deeper issues.

First we must define what a choir is, then begin to say clearly what the role of the choir is in the life of the church. A *choir* is a group of people dedicated to fostering and helping lead the gathered community in expressing its faith through sung prayer. The *role* of the choir was enunciated in a speech by the late Fr. Eugene Walsh who said, "The choir's three functions are to first of all lead the assembly's song, then to provide embellishment to things the assembly does well, and to do things beautifully that the assembly cannot do for itself." I have never forgotten those words. They are exquisitely clear, and lay out the roles of a choir in order of their importance. We can examine our celebrational consciences as to whether we have placed more value on one function over another, or have honored them in opposite order. We should always remember that one of the primary ways an assembly learns to be an assembly is in singing together. The unifying power of common singing should never be underestimated.

Next we must consider hospitality, a term we hear a lot about in the church today. Hospitality is infinitely more complex than juice and cookies or coffee after Mass! Hospitality within our ministry begins among the choir members themselves. It means that we go out of our way for one another, making an intentional effort to care for one another, making a clear sign to the assembly of what the music of faith does for us. The presence of hospitality among us is to be seen throughout the week, not just on Sunday. This makes it imperative that we make rehearsals—on time and ready to work. Choir members are part of a team that counts on each member's presence and our effort as director. Not to be at a rehearsal, or to come unprepared, is inhospitable. When we come together to work—to practice as a team—we are saying, "Yes, this is important, and we want things to be right for the Sunday liturgy." Good will is not enough; practice is necessary. Hospitality within the choir spills over and truly makes possible the choir's experience of hospitality, both musically and humanly, with the rest of the Sunday assembly.

The loving response of a hospitable person, mixed with the discipline of one who knows the joy of making music, makes a marvelous member of a church choir. The final element in the equation is the faith of that singer, the personal faith that gets expressed through the music and in the hospitality called for by the "Law of Love" of the Gospel. So many times in the years I have been in this work I have heard it said and watched it happen: Being in the choir becomes a conversion experience in the faith life of the singer. Initially each person comes to choir for her or his own reasons. Let's take a look at the main kinds of motivations we can observe as people join the choir:

A. A singer often comes to the church choir first for the music. A singer sometimes comes just to sing or with a secret hope of a solo. These singers can easily have their expectations met by a competent director.
B. Some singers come for social reasons, knowing that their friendship circle will increase, and that they will have a new and important support group. These singers almost always get their needs met because shared music experiences bond people together extraordinarily.
C. A desire for a deeper prayer life motivates some singers to join the choir. These members see joining the choir as a way of deepening their prayer life. Membership for them is like being part of a prayer group. They tend to find music as an important means, but the end is always the prayer.
D. Some singers come because they feel called to "do something" for the church, to give of themselves in time and talent. These generous singers enjoy the music and join in the hospitality, but they hold within themselves another place by which they measure their success. These singers will find satisfaction in the very fact of being there, at both rehearsal and on Sunday. These singers tend to take the lead in the relationship the choir holds with the rest of the assembly on Sunday.

Many people have a combination of two or more of these reasons for being a choir member. What is more, the reason a person may have had for joining the choir may be quite different from the reason why they are a member five years later. Maybe it was the music that brought him or her in but it is the social interaction that keeps one coming back. In the end the goal will be to have all members see the value of and to some degree participate in all of these motivations. This is what makes for a well-rounded choir member. Here is a brief checklist of expectations for choir members that offers one means of developing these aspects:

1. Dedication to the task: Good music, in all forms, requires regular effort by all the participants.
2. Regular attendance: Being on time and ready to work are necessities for all, each week.
3. Being a team player: Giving up self-will for the good of the whole group.
4. Spirituality: Maintaining an attitude of openness and prayer.

This checklist may seem simplistic, very nuts and bolts, but consider them in the context of Fr. William Bauman's definition of ministry: "…service rendered out of love, and with a deep respect for the person served, after the model of Jesus."[1] Herein lies the beginning of the conversion experience that almost inevitably happens to people who commit themselves to the ministry of the choir. It is the "model of Jesus" that becomes so increasingly clear as we sing our theology in the text and notes of the music for worship. We are confronted with what we believe about him, and our faith lives change as we sing with our sisters and brothers who are also courageously allowing their faith lives to be changed.

---

1 *The Ministry of Music,* 2nd edition (Washington, D.C: Litugical Conference, 1979) 7.

It often takes more than we originally expected, as we realize what the ministry of the choir really is. We know it when we hear it and feel it. There is no event more thrilling than the sound of good singing with the assembly. We continue to pile up memories of what it was like to sing that special anthem or concert as a choir and have that profound silence that comes to the room after the last note is sung, a moment that happens in the body, the mind, and the heart. It carries us to a place where words alone can never take us. It is a special sign of unity, of oneness of faith and spirit. We know that to get there means that we have spent much of ourselves to bring the moment to truth. If you are new to this ministry, realize that there will be many days when all the effort on your part will not be enough; after all the moment of so musical a communion is a gift like any other. We prepare and do all we can to receive it, but we cannot cause it to be given. This is service, ministry and discipline, embraced by faith and by music. It is the yeast in the dough, the leavening agent of the larger community, and it is "after the model of Jesus."

Why sing in the choir? So that our brothers and sisters in our parish communities might write to us as Paul wrote to the Philippians: "I thank my God in all my remembrance of you, always in every prayer of mine, thankful for your partnership in the gospel, from the first day until now." (Phil. 1:3, 5)

Part ONE:

The Place for the Choir and Preparing to Direct the Choir

A choir director is asked to take people, arrange them in a space and have them produce sound in time as prayer. This first section deals with everything that affects you and your singers before you begin any rehearsal. The basics of organizing space and gaining the needed information to conduct singers are thus at the foundation of the work of the ministry of directing a choir. Whether you are an experienced director or brand new, this section will help you to appreciate the basic configuration of space and the approach to preparing to sing that will give a solid base upon which to build.

Singing from the Same Page

Chapter 1

Today's music directors have a great myriad of responsibilities to attend to and have to function as persons of detail each and every day. In our haste to get the job done, we sometimes lose sight of what it means to be producers of musical craft or of musical art. What does it mean to make good craft? The first time I ever heard the word craft in relation to music, all I could think of was the image of a person with long, nimble fingers working straw into a basket. It seemed effortless; that basket was being carefully formed by those skilled hands that turned ordinary elements into a work of art. It took me some years to see the relationship between basket making and music, but I eventually came to realize that musical elements are in some ways ordinary elements themselves, and that each time they are formed by skilled hands, ears and voices, music, too, becomes art.

Now, if art seems too fancy a word to use in choir directing, then perhaps we need a definition of what art is. According to Mr. Webster, and he is very exacting, art is a noun which means "skill; human skill as opposed to nature; skill applied to music, painting, poetry, etc." Art is not a term to shy away from, but to embrace fully at the service of all God's people. Music making ranks right up there as the highest of the fine arts because it so quickly and readily ministers to the human spirit. So from the start we need to be clear that what we are doing is more than sound production. Music is shaping and joining various sounds with the goal of changing human hearts, of making people aware of the presence of the divine and helping them respond to that presence. I hope that gives your choral attitude a whole new dimension of how important your detailed work is. We all know that music can take us to

importance

the farthest reaches of the human heart, and can speak to us more powerfully and profoundly than the spoken word alone ever could. Music is the soul's own poetry; it is a gift from God, perhaps the very sound of God.

Often when we hear a world class pianist or other artist who moves us to our feet in a standing ovation, we think, WOW! What marvelous technique they have. Though our choirs may never sing in one of the world's great concert halls, every choir, your choir, can sing with a certain amount of technique that is both satisfying and artful as we minister to our assemblies week after week.

For every choir, large or small, some parameters must be set for working together if everyone is to truly sing from the same page and achieve this level of artistry. I base my own choir's work on two basic premises before we ever get to the music. These "cardinal rules" are based on a simple understanding of choral technique. As a very young piano student, I was fortunate enough to have a fine piano teacher who was fond of having us recite definitions at our regular exam periods. She taught that "technique" was intelligently guided muscle power. For singers I like to think of technique as intelligently guided vocal ability. It is a simple way to view it, and I'm always looking for simple ways to communicate not so simple things. It is important for directors, and more importantly for choirs, to realize that good technique is NOT about the art of the perfect in choral singing, but about the art of the possible. From this flows the two premises:

Premise 1: What is done must be done together. This applies to every aspect of corporate musical life. There is no one person who is more important than the next, and all agree to form a corporate voice when singing together as a choir. Everyone sings vowels the same way, counts the same way, etc, etc, etc.

Premise 2: Anything not under control of the individual singer is to be considered a vocal weakness, not a strength. For example: Is everyone always using good breath control or do high notes always have to be loud? Does everyone know that difficult measure in Sunday's anthem?

What these premises teach is that all must constantly strive for great teamwork so that everyone can sing together as a single unit. When people sing in the choir, they sing as a part of the ensemble, and they must work in total harmony for the benefit of the common good.

Space

Chapter 2

Now that we are in agreement about our task and how we will begin to carry it out, it is time "to plan our work and work our plan" and the first step toward that is to get organized. I hope you are lucky enough to have a choir room. In some situations it may be "dreaming the impossible dream," but a regular space to rehearse in is very important to the care and feeding of choirs. It is a place where we teach, learn, pray, laugh and cry as we prepare to lead the Sunday liturgy each week. Rehearsing in the church every now and then is fine, but can often be too distracting for the real work we need to do, and learning to listen is often negated by the great or not so great acoustics of a large room. What is more, rehearsing in an empty church can give a false sense of volume, since the presence of a church full of people radically changes the acoustics of the space. So, try to find some little space to call your own, at least on rehearsal night and Sunday warm-up time. It too, will become sacred space, and the benefits are many.

While you will do the best with whatever space you can find, an ideal choir room would have the following attributes:

Reverberation. Acoustical engineers speak of how "live" a room is, and while there are meters that can measure this, you can get a relative idea of how live a room is by simply clapping your hands once and then timing how long the echo of the sound lasts. An echo of 2–3 seconds is ideal. Anything shorter and your singers will not be able to hear each other well; anything longer and your singers might be lulled into a false notion of how strong their sound actually is. Check the room in several places to make sure that it is relatively constant.

Lighting. Hymnals and sheet music are known for trying to include as much information as possible in a limited space. Because this will often lead to a smaller font size on the page, it is crucial that your choir room has adequate lighting. Natural lighting is wonderful, but since you will be using the room in the evening, at least for weekly choir practices, you will need to have a well-lit room. When you first take over a choir room, it is worth the expense to have a technician come in with a light meter to make sure that the lights are bright enough for the singers to read their music comfortably. This also applies to the space where the choir and all the assembly sing during liturgy. Use of additional lamps as needed will help keep your choir members (and you!) from growing tired just because of the strain on your eyes from dim lighting.

Risers or No? The use of platforms to raise the second and subsequent rows of singers is an interesting issue. The advantage of being better able to see and hear the back rows of your choir needs to be balanced against the setting that the choir will find itself in during the liturgy. The use of risers in a liturgical space is to be discouraged because it tends to indicate that the choir is a performing group that is only to be listened to. This is not the goal of a liturgical choir. The decision, then comes down to whether or not you gain sufficient benefit from better seeing and hearing your choir during rehearsal times to outweigh the difficulty that can be caused from singing in a different arrangement during the liturgy.

Chairs. Since the choir is standing for most of the music sung during the liturgy, it is not crucial to have the same type of seating in the church as in the rehearsal space. Seating for the choir should be comfortable, because singers are going to be seated for a good part of the time during rehearsals, but more importantly it should encourage good posture (see chapter 9). A final criterion is that the chairs in the choir room should not be flimsy. For all these reasons, this means that folding chairs are not generally acceptable. Good quality chairs can be expensive, but they are an important element in supporting the ministry of the choir members.

Choir Folder Storage. Whether you use binders or folders, you need a place to store them. Custom designed shelving, perhaps built by a member of the choir or even by another parishioner works best. In this way the shelves are the right size for the needed resources and can be numbered so that each choir member can mark his or her music and be sure to get the same folio each time a piece is sung.

Keyboard. If the choir is supported by a keyboard instrument, it is not usually possible to have the same instrument in both the choir room and the church. Still, the sound of the keyboard that supports the singing in the choir room should produce a sound that will approximate the volume and timbre of the sound the choir will hear during the liturgy. Most often a piano or electronic keyboard is used in the choir room, while an organ and piano are found in the church. The instrumentalist needs to adjust the way music is played so that the singers will feel the same kind of support during rehearsal as during the liturgy.

Your Place. Once the singers are arranged, consider where you should position yourself. As a basic rule, you should conduct from the same relative place and elevation that you will be occupying in the liturgy. There are two exceptions to this rule. First, one might not have an ideal place to conduct from in church. In this case use a better position in the choir room, with better sight lines and acoustics. The other exception is when one needs to work with specific parts of the choir. Choir directors should have the flexibility to move around as they address different issues in a rehearsal. For this reason they might not want to stand on an elevated platform, even if they conduct from such a place during the liturgy.

Place for Other Instrumentalists. When a choir is supported by an instrument other than the organ or when additional instruments are used, the relative volume of its sound in the choir room will be much stronger than in the church. If the instruments are played at full volume or placed directly in front of the choir during rehearsal, singers may come to rely on a specific sound that will not be as clear in church. It is important to ensure that these instruments are placed off to the side and/or that they be played in such a way that the overall effect will be as close as possible to what will be heard during the liturgy.

Music Library. All of the music resources: choral, instrumental, sheet music or in book form should be easily accessible, either in the choir room or in the office space used by the choir director (sometimes this is the same space). Sheet music is easily stored in hanging folders, so there needs to be enough filing cabinets for the current library and sufficient shelf space for all the director's book and recording resources. In addition, there should be room to allow for the growth in collections and an archival space to store music that is no longer part of the active repertoire.

Place for Coats, Purses, Winter Clothing. One of the most basic elements of any religious enterprise is hospitality. No matter what else happens during the rehearsal period, it is essential that singers feel like the choir room is designed to welcome them. Make certain that there are places to hang coats, especially in the winter.

Climate Control. It would be ideal, if usually impossible, to have an independent climate control for the choir room. Often this will be the only room in the church plant being used, and if there is a computerized system that turns the furnace or air conditioning down at night, the choir room could become very uncomfortable indeed.

Restroom Facilities. This matter of basic hospitality is often overlooked, but an ideal setting would have restroom facilities available immediately adjacent to or at least on the same floor as the choir room. Proper lighting needs to be provided so that singers feel safe in going to use these facilities.

Water Cooler. Singing dries out the throat, as the ubiquitous water bottles that choir members tote with them testify. For this reason, a source of cold water should be a normal feature of a choir room.

Mirror. Choir members will appreciate having a full-length mirror available to them. While this ministry is not a fashion show, such a mirror will allow the singers to feel confident that they are presentable for the ministry they will perform.

Storage for Robes (if Used) and Instruments. While robing is a matter of custom and taste for choirs, they are used in some places, at least for more important feasts. Choirs that have them, need to have a decent storage place for them and a means for ensuring that they are cleaned and pressed on a regular basis. As for hand bells, percussion and other instruments that the church might own, having them lying around the choir room can give the space a claustrophobic feel to it. Have a place for everything and put everything in its place.

Recording/Technology Facilities. While foreign to most choir directors, the use of recording facilities are becoming a standard tool to help choirs develop their sound. An audio record of a choir can be very discouraging if done too soon while learning a piece of music, but once your choir has gotten the basic tone down, recordings can be useful in fine tuning the sound. Recording rehearsals is also a good way for the director to check for problem areas that might have escaped notice during the rehearsal. For more difficult pieces, recording equipment (including a tape duplication system) can also allow directors to provide members of the choir with recordings of their part to listen to during the week. A video record of rehearsal can also be instructive for directors as they develop their own abilities, especially if they share the video with a trusted colleague. Finally, there are more advanced technologies that allow a director to have a speaker behind each section of the choir playing only that section's part. While teaching tools such as this are still beyond the budget of most choirs, having space and wiring provided for these developments will allow one to take advantage of them as they become accessible.

Security. A choir room needs to be secure. Singers will leave their valuables in the room while they minister in the worship space, and there is an increasing amount of valuable technology and instruments stored there. Make sure that there is a good lock on the door, and then use it.

Seating. If possible, I suggest that seating be arranged in the rehearsal space (if separate) to mimic the seating in the worship space. In my own choir room the singers are arranged the same way as when we sing in the church, which is of great value, because then my singers can rely on hearing the same blending of voices. Nothing throws singers off more quickly than hearing strange voices singing different parts than what they heard in rehearsal. At the same time, do not become too complacent. I often change the arrangement of the choir for certain musical effects, for example when two voices will share a line of music or when they need to hear each other in order to hear their own notes or rhythms. Still, as a norm, the basic seating charts that follow are ones that I have found especially useful.

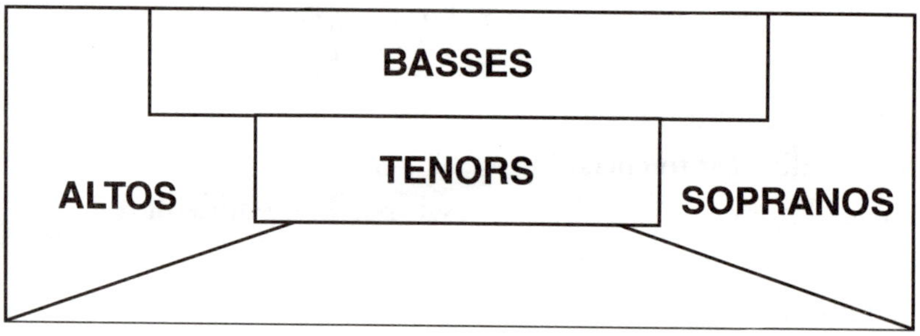

In this type of setup the sopranos and basses (outer voices) and the altos and tenors (inner voices) are strategically placed to allow one to listen for the balance of the voices and their harmony. This is only one way to set up seating. A three-part ensemble might look like this:

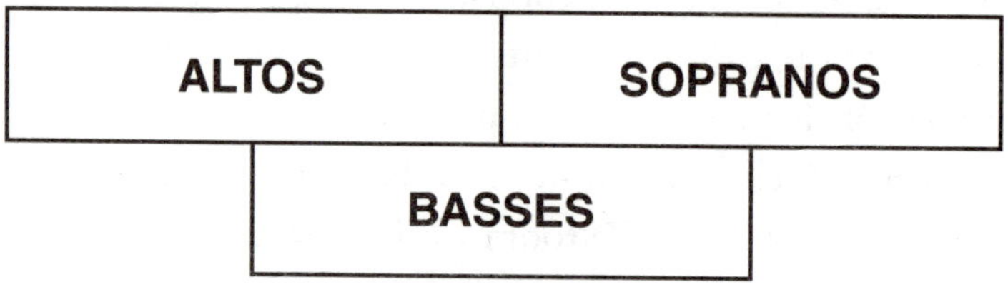

There are many ways to set up seating arrangements so find a "basic seating plan" that works for you and your choir. Depending on the strength of various sections, the sight lines and a whole raft of other issues, adjust the seating of the choir to match the situation. It is part of the discipline that says, "I've thought about our voices, and I care about what we do as an ensemble." Try to duplicate this in the church. If your current seating doesn't work, and you know whether it does or not, try to fix it! Good sight lines are necessary for the singers, especially if the director plays and directs at the same time. Don't be afraid to re-arrange. I have a friend who plays and directs, whose choir sits in a space angled just enough from the organ console that most of the singers have no sight line at all to that console; an impossible situation that week after week sabotages the poor choir. The bottom line is that singers need to be able to hear each other in order to join their tone to the whole, and choir directors and their singers need good sight lines so that the directors can lead the singers and shape the music they make.

Chapter 3

Organization and Paperwork

I cannot stress enough the importance of good planning and record keeping. The only way the director will know what resources are at disposal and what is possible is to have good records. This applies to sheet music and song books; it applies to musical instruments and solo instrumentalists, but it also applies to people. It applies to the singers in the choir and to the director and his or her use of time.

Organizing Your Time

Get a Franklin planner and a copy of Stephen Covey's marvelous book, *The Seven Habits of Highly Effective People*. Read it and re-read it! Choir directors must be organized and set realistic goals in order to accomplish their tasks. Only then can they move through the choir year confidently, building good blocks upon good blocks. The use of the planner also creates a chronicle of how your goals become realities. Good records of what you wanted to achieve and what the choir was able to accomplish will be a valuable resource as you move forward. Some choirs learn music quickly, but need more time to review it each time the piece comes up. Others are slower at learning new music but better at picking it up again after several weeks or months. The choir director's goal is to learn how the choir works and to plan accordingly.

Organizing Your Repertoire

Liturgy planning sheets are another essential resource for developing and evaluating the music used at the liturgy. A set of sheets that detail what has been sung over the past year with notes describing how difficult it was for the choir or assembly to learn is a valuable resource when planning the coming liturgical season or the entire year. I keep my Liturgy/Music planning forms in my planner. It is always with me so that if I think of some little detail, no matter where I am, I can write it down. My Liturgy/Music form fits my planner perfectly and looks like this:

SUNDAY MUSIC PLAN

SUNDAY/FEAST____________________DATE ______________

PRELUDE ____

MUSIC: ____

THE PROCESSION ____________________________________

PENITENTIAL/SPRINKLING RITE ________________________

GLORIA____

THE PSALM ____

GOSPEL ACCLAMATION _________________

INTERCESSIONS – SUNG____________OR SPOKEN__________

ANTHEM ______________________________

HOLY, MEMORIAL ACCLAMATION, AMEN _____

LAMB OF GOD _______________________________________

COMMUNION HYMN ___________________________________

CHORAL ____

HYMN OF THANKSGIVING _____________________________

CONCLUDING VOLUNTARY _____________________________

SPECIAL NOTES:

Feel free to reproduce this form, or better yet, design your own. Oregon Catholic Press has a great planning form in *Today's Liturgy*. Special forms for weddings and other such liturgies are available on the company's website www.ocp.org). Incidentally, I also keep wedding planning forms in my binder along with all the other details of my life. One final thought about planning:

What happens on a given Sunday morning when both tenors are out sick? It is very important that directors have a "Plan B" set of unison, two- or three- part anthems at their fingertips so that their not madly scrambling around for something to sing at the last minute. As choirs learn these reserve works, let them know that one of the reasons for learning these pieces is for unexpected situations when some of them or even you are suddenly sick or unable to be present. This will help them to appreciate the importance of these works that might seem more simple than what they usually sing.

Know Each Voice

Another important part of being organized is to know your voices. In church choir work, directors are always thrilled to welcome new members who selflessly give their time and talents in service to others. The responsibilities to these special volunteers are many, but none is more important than knowing their voices and what they are capable of. I like to spend three to five minutes with every new member as they join the choir and with the other members once or twice a year doing a vocal check up. It helps me to learn what these voices can do and helps in section placement. By maintaining some individual profile sheets, I have lots of information about each singer and the development of their voice over time at my fingertips. This will be especially helpful in recognizing serious changes in voices over time. My Choir Member Profile sheets look like this:

Office of Sacred Music
Oliver Douberly, Director

CHOIR MEMBER PROFILE

(this part to be filled out by the choir member)

NAME ______________________________ TODAY'S DATE ____________

ADDRESS ______________________________ PHONE ____________

____

BUSINESS PHONE: ____________________ DATE OF BIRTH ____________

SPOUSE'S (OTHER'S) NAME: ______________________________

MUSICAL DATA

PREVIOUS MUSICAL EXPERIENCE: ______________________________

____

- -

(this part to be filled out by the choir director)

PART(S) PREVIOUSLY SUNG: S1 S2 A1 A2 T1 T2 B1 B2 OTHER ________

RANGE ____________________ VOICE TIMBRE: S A T B

____

____

____

____

COMMENTS: ____

____

____

QUALITY: 1 2 3 4 5

INTONATION: 1 2 3 4 5

SIGHT READING: 1 2 3 4 5

PART ASSIGNED: S1 S2
A1 A2
T1 T2
B1 B2

Again, feel free to copy this, or make up your own.

The vocal check up goes like this:

1. Have each member sing something like "America, the Beautiful," or "O Come, O Come Emmanuel," checking for general breathing and breath support, and their sound in general.
2. Check range by vocalizing each person using a five-note descending scale on the vowel "ah." Vocalize up and down the scale to find their lowest and highest "good notes" as well as where each person's breaks occur.

3. Vocalize for good vowel sounds using the same five-note descending scale on the vowel sounds: "Ma, May, Me, Mo, Mu."
4. Ask them to sight-read a short line of music that includes the interval of a fourth. The leap of a fourth is often tricky for volunteer singers.

This is a very simple process which takes only a few minutes to complete and you can schedule these interviews, perhaps four or five at a time, ten to fifteen minutes before the week-night rehearsal. Of course this means that you are always prepared well in advance for your rehearsals. It could be counter-productive to rush through a vocal check up in order to finish your preparations for that night's rehearsal. Record your information on the Choir Member Profile sheets, and discuss with the singer any major changes that occur. I find that my singers really appreciate the care and the individual attention.

Organizing the Choir Library

Chapter 4

Organizing a choir library can be a slow and arduous task, especially if there are lots of titles and they have not been put into any sort of arrangement for a long time. It is a considerable investment of time and energy, but will be well worth the effort. Here is one way to organize music so that one is not digging around at the last minute trying to remember where something is:

1. Take a complete inventory of everything. Include title, composer, publisher, how many copies or any other pertinent note.
2. Create categories for the music; these could include:
   - Mass Settings
   - Ritual Music
   - Psalms
   - Choral Anthems/Octavos
   - Major Works
3. First make a reference list by title, and decide what goes in each category. Don't alphabetize at this point.
4. Give all pieces a manila folder and include title and category number, such as
   - MS 15—followed by the name of the mass setting
   - O 40—followed by the name of the octavo
   - MW 20—followed by the name of the major work
5. Store in filing cabinets according to number and category.
6. Create a master index by title and category, then cross reference by composer, alphabetical, etc. and keep a copy of this on your desk and in the location where the music is stored.
7. Update the listings each time a new item is added.

This is but one way of organizing a choir library and you will no doubt want to devise a system that works well for you. Easy retrieval and storage are paramount, and knowing your resources and how to access them is the goal. A cautionary word about copyrights is in order here. It is often tempting to make copies for something for immediate use, but unless you've composed it or the piece is in public domain, DO NOT COPY someone else's music. It is the same as stealing and we must be vigilant about this if there is to be justice in this matter. The copyright laws are clear and any good publisher will be happy to share that information. Composers and writers work hard to produce wonderful published materials and it is our responsibility to see that their efforts are protected and respected.

A Choir Librarian

Finding someone to serve as choir librarian can be an invaluable asset to your work and if you sound the call, someone will usually come forward. It must be the right person—someone who is personally organized and likes to work with details. It is a big job and might include the following tasks:

1. Distributes and collects after use, all octavos and other pieces sung by the choir making sure that it is returned to the proper file.
2. Sees that the music is kept in good order, in it's folders and in the right place.
3. Keeps the indexes up to date: alphabetical, numerical and by composer. Makes new entries as they are added to the choir library.
4. Takes attendance and notifies the director of unexcused absences so that the director may follow up.
5. Keeps a neat bulletin board up to date with announcements and notices of upcoming events, schedules and member news.

Keeping Track of Instrumentalists

Chapter 5

Instrumentalists are an important resource for the choir director. Not only do they add to more solemn celebrations such as Easter and Christmas, they can also be a great help in the week-to-week work of this ministry. A trumpet heard all through the Easter season or a flute or oboe all through Advent can help bind these weeks together. It is one of the ways to support the work of the liturgy commission in your parish. If you are one of the many choir directors who conducts while playing at the keyboard, having a resource of keyboard players to draw upon for some of the more complicated liturgies of the year or in case of holidays or emergencies is very important indeed.

In all except the largest cities, there is a limited supply of professional players, and a network among them. Finding and keeping good players happens over time. Your task as choir director is to make sure that you have a plan for when you intend to use instrumentalists throughout the year, based upon the liturgical and financial constraints of your parish, and then hire them early. Make sure you confirm every booking (including fees) in writing, and keep the players' personal information (including social security numbers) in a secure place. Given the frequency of identity theft, it is advisable that a locked file cabinet or the parish safe be used to keep this information. Do not pay instrumentalists "under the table" because it is not legal or professional. We expect a professional musician to perform a professional service, and anything that would undermine that professionalism is not appropriate.

In almost every parish there are people who play instruments and will volunteer to play for church. These offers must be handled with great care. With the exception of children's choirs (see David Nastal's great book in the BASICS series, *Children's Choir* OCP 11126 PQ) where the playing of instruments may form part of the ministry of choir members, in the liturgy there is no room for musicians who are not able to support the song of the assembly. You should audition anyone who wants to offer their services as an instrumentalist. Make it clear that rejection does not necessarily mean that you do not appreciate their talent, but rather that their talent may not lend itself to supporting the song of a choir and an assembly at prayer. Do keep a welcoming eye out for musicians in your parish, especially those who may be away at college pursuing a music degree. They will be home for Christmas and perhaps Easter, just when you need them most.

When you identify players who are able and willing to work with you, create files for them. Plan and book them well in advance, keeping copies of each booking confirmation letter you send in their file. If possible, rely on the same musicians for the same celebrations from one year to the next. This will make your planning easier and over time will establish a relationship between the player and the choir. They will get to know each other's style and work with each other to develop a more unified sound.

Finally, keep a list of emergency keyboard players. This should include not only those people who do not have a regular weekend gig, but also those who might be able to get away for a specific Sunday or in an emergency because the liturgy for which they play is at a different time from your own. Also include retired organists on this list. When the keyboard player (whether you or someone else) is sick, a competent player is all that is needed. You might have to simplify your plan for the day (see chapter 3) but your choir will still be able to serve by leading the song of the church. And that is the point.

The Importance of Personal Preparation

Chapter 6

As choir directors, one of the important roles that we take on by the very nature of the ministry is that of teacher. Our choirs depend on us week after week to lead them in an ongoing process to learn musicianship and what it means to practice well. There is simply no substitute for knowing what you are doing and being personally prepared. No amount of good will or well-intentioned effort will compensate. Your choir members know when you do not "have it together." There are lots of ways to prepare for rehearsal and I believe the more detailed and specific (yes, bar by bar) we can be, the better the results. It is important to work on repertoire several weeks in advance, especially with a volunteer choir. There is something good that happens when we spread the learning process out over a period of time that is important to every choir's growth. It also affords the director an opportunity to "live with" that music in such a way that often reveals issues that must be dealt with that are usually not apparent at first reading. We must teach our singers what it is they have to have under control. They must mark their individual scores in pencil as per your directions. Therefore, your preparation and score study are imperative to their success.

As you begin your study of a piece, some general observations should be made. These should always be passed on to the choir in non-technical terms.

Overall Form—Note the phrasing and mark rehearsal numbers or letters to specific measures (perhaps every ten bars).

Style—A knowledge of general music styles such as Renaissance, Baroque, and Romantic will tell you what kind of tone to use with a particular piece. We don't sing Palestrina, for instance, with the same tone that we sing Brahms.

Dynamics and Shading—Indicated and non-indicated need to be considered from the very first moment. Don't learn a piece with the choir with the idea that you will add the dynamics later. They are a rhythmic part of the equation.

Tempo—Often this is not indicated and we must make the decision based on our ability to negotiate cleanly the smallest unit of time.

Singing each line—This enables us to pick out the "tunes" as they appear in the different voice parts, shows us the problem intervals, and helps us set the phrasing and articulations.

Diction—Analyze difficult words so that they become rhythmic and don't distort the given rhythm of the music.

Accompaniment—Is it duet style where the choir is the other partner, or a simple harmonic fill-in?

Instruments—Know where to cue well in advance and mark those spots.

These are general, overall considerations that seem important to begin with. If we want to be more specific, consider the following. It is part of your discipline and these items will help to improve you own musicianship.

A. Do a brief harmonic analysis and consider:
   - Chordal structure—this helps reveal the form
   - Important key changes
   - Tonal centers
   - Leaps of a perfect fourth and major thirds—difficult intervals
   - Thematic and non-thematic material

- Harmonic rhythm—rhythm patterns caused by changes in harmony

  When there are few chord changes (slow harmonic rhythm) a quicker tempo may be used. When there are many chord changes in a row (fast harmonic rhythm), a slower tempo is needed.

B. Do a brief rhythmic analysis and consider:

- Basic meter and pulse—make sure you can count every part, every line
- Changes of meter with a given piece
- Phrasing of each part and points of arrival or important beats
- Breaths, lifts, and changes in speed (e.g. *rit. accel.*)
- Problem words—look for those sounds that are more difficult to sing

C. Dynamic analysis

- Dynamics as indicated by the composer
- Non indicated dynamics- those revealed by the pulse
- Over the bar ties that can cause rhythmic problems

D. Textual analysis

- Vowel check; especially note all diphthongs
- Vowel modification—depending on the range of the singers some vowels must be changed so as not to sound forced. For instance an "e" vowel sung on a very high note may have to be sung as an "ah" to keep it from sounding offensive
- Note all problem consonants and negotiate rhythmically

It is very helpful to color code specific details in a score so that they can be seen at a glance ahead of time. The color-coding idea I got from a student of Margaret Hillis of the Chicago Symphony Chorus many years ago and it has served me well. Try it; it will save you lots of precious moments in rehearsal. Be as neat and precise as you can be. We can call this "knowing the score." It is very helpful to learn (practice) to hear directly from the score without the piano, other instrument or recordings. In this way the interpretation becomes more original and the creative process is sparked. Try to make the score come to life in your ear; it will make further analysis easier and quicker.

RED indicates an increase in either dynamics or tempo and includes the words crescendo, accelerando, or others such as *piu mosso,* which are underlined.

RED also indicates "F" for loud (circle it), or fast for metronome markings of a quarter that equal 100 or more (drawn with a box around it).

BROWN indicates moderate dynamics and tempi and is also used for accents. Circle for "mf," underlines for words such as *moderato* and boxes for metronome markings of a quarter that equal 80–100.

BLUE indicates a decrease in dynamics or tempo, marked the same way. Also use for *ritard* or terms like *meno mosso* that are underlined. Use also to indicated soft or "p" in a circle or slow for metronome markings of a quarter that equal 42–80.

GREEN is used for "pp" or less and marked in the same way.

You may wish to experiment and come up with your own color scheme for marking your scores. In any event, it is a very helpful process, especially if you are preparing an orchestral score. The goal is to be able to give yourself cues so that you will pass on to your singers all the cues they will need to sing with confidence.

Ready, Set....

Chapter 7

Two final areas of concern are attendance and music reading skills. How you approach these will strongly affect the self-esteem of your choir members and the importance that your singers place on the ministry they do. If attendance is not considered an important element, those members who come faithfully may become discouraged. When it comes to the skill of reading music, you will need to balance the skill level of your choir with the amount of time you will need to invest to achieve a level of fluency in reading music that will make for an efficient rehearsal time. Both of these issues deal with the tension between accepting people as they come to us and making the most of our time together. As a choir director you need to balance the real-life situations of your singers with the real need to cover a certain amount of music. Without this balance you will likely get the feeling that the choir is out of control.

Some Important Words about Attendance

It often takes a few years for a choir to solidify as a group whose members are consistently present at rehearsals and services, and that time of development can be frustrating. Good people come and go, families get relocated, and others, though many may be fine singers, over-estimate their ability to make a weekly commitment. Don't give up! Those are problems that occur any time one works with volunteers and are inherent to the system. Be thankful for the regular group that comes and align your plans to fit their capabilities so that they sound good and know it. It is also important that the director foster personal relationships, not necessarily to be best friends with everyone in the choir, but to be truly caring and appreciative to all present.

Good attendance happens when:

It becomes a habit over time.
The choir members take pride in themselves as a significant ministry within the parish.
Everyone understands and accepts the expectations necessary for choir membership.
The choir director learns to become "pastor" to the choir community.
The choir community feels appreciated by parish, pastor and the assembly.
All members share a unity of purpose for the greater good.

Rote vs. Note Teaching

One of the great challenges of working with the volunteer choir is that not everyone comes to the choir with equal note-reading skills. It often becomes necessary, especially if you are starting a new choir, to use a certain amount of teaching music by rote. This might allow you to teach a lot of music quickly and can be a helpful aid to ear training. As one of our roles as music directors involves being the choral teacher of the choir, it is desirable to find a way to teach music reading skills to our choirs and to develop their overall sense of musicianship. This is an investment of time, but is well worth the effort. You might consider offering a four-to-six week mini-course on the subject and perhaps schedule it for thirty minutes before the rehearsal. It might also be a part of an existing adult education series. Most choir members develop the desire early on to become better skilled over time and that certainly includes the ability to read music at a basic level. You will be amazed at how quickly this endeavor will benefit the whole group and it will go a long way toward laying a solid foundation for the choir.

Part TWO:

The Rehearsal

Now that we are well on our way to being organized, the music has been distributed, and we've studied our scores, we are ready to consider the rehearsal. It is crucial that they start on time, every time, regardless of who is there. People who are habitually tardy will eventually get the message that if they are late, they will miss much. Of course, there are always exceptions to every rule, but in general this works well for me. A well-paced, well-planned rehearsal should be one of our major weekly goals. It is a special time in the life of the choir, for obvious reasons, but it also can be a moment for building and deepening faith. Very often singers come to rehearsal fatigued and worn out from a busy day. A good rehearsal, where good breathing habits are practiced and sitting and standing are alternated, can serve to refresh and stimulate tired muscles and minds. I like to begin every rehearsal with a written plan. The better organized you are, the more you will accomplish. Focus on results and plan to cover four to six weeks of repertoire at any given rehearsal. Do this by working the difficult sections of all pieces with only a light review of their easy parts. By stretching out the learning process the challenging sections will have time to settle and will become much easier. My own rehearsal planning sheet always consists of:

1. Preparing to sing: Prayer, Posture and Breathing
2. Warm up—no more than five or ten minutes
3. Hymns (every verse!) and service music
4. Six weeks of choral repertoire
5. Announcements and closing prayer

Your choir members can help keep the rehearsal moving at a good pace. Ask the singers to refrain from asking questions or interrupting while you are in a teaching moment. Ask for questions at the end of the moment, section or piece in order to ensure that material that needs to be covered will be, efficiently and in good time.

Chapter 8

Prayer

It is the role of the music director to unify the group by teaching, training, and leading by example. For instance, the choir is not likely to pray together if the choir director doesn't first pray with them. Leading a group in prayer requires a personal prayer life. If you do not pray on your own on a regular basis, it will be harder to lead your singers in prayer in a genuine manner. Prayer needs to be a regular part of your day so that you have a source from which to draw when you lead your choir in prayer. A regular, common prayer life is a very important unifying element in forming the community of the choir. Remember that choirs take their cues from their directors; that person sets the tone for the attitude of the whole choir from the outset. Prayer together is the foundation of everything we do; it is our reason for being there in the first place. It is important that we start and end with prayer at every gathering so that we stay centered on who we are as Christian people. In this way, we give witness to our faith and set an example for the larger community by our very attitude.

There are a number of very good resources which provide prayers for choirs. Lawrence Johnson's *A Singer's Companion to the Church Year* (three volumes) gives suggested prayers for each week of the liturgical year. Jeanne Hunt's *Choir Prayers* and *More Choir Prayers* are great collections of prayers for different events in the life of the choir. The psalm of the Sunday for which you are preparing was chosen in light of the first reading and ultimately the gospel of the day; often this will provide you with a great prayer for the choir. The Sacramentary also provides collect prayers (opening prayer, prayer over the gifts and prayer after Communion) that help focus us on the liturgy of the day. These collects generally follow a standard form which you can use in devising your own prayers.

Flexibility in prayer is important because there will be times when choir rehearsals will fall on days when important events are happening in the world or in your choir. At such times your storehouse of prayers may not suffice. In such a case, you can easily develop your own prayer by following the collect structure. These prayers begin by naming God. If there has been some disaster, you might call on God as "our protector" or if a choir member has just found out that he or she has cancer you might call God "our healer." The second part of the collect structure is to name some great thing that God has done. The action of God you cite should be based on the way you have called on God. If you have invoked God as "source of life" because one of your singers has announced that she is pregnant, you could then cite one of the times that God granted a child to someone, such as "in your goodness you gave the gift of a child to Rachel and your own son to Mary." The third part of the prayer is to ask God to continue this pattern of blessing. If you have called on God as a healer and mentioned the healing of the paralytic lowered through the roof, then you could ask God to grant health to all who suffer, and especially to the member who is absent. You could then expand the prayer to ask that all our music be a source of support and healing to the people to whom we minister. The last part of the collect structure is to make the prayer through Christ our Lord.

One other issue with regard to prayer is who should lead the prayer. There is clearly no one answer to this question, and the answer does not have to be the same every time you gather. You, as leader, should certainly lead prayer sometimes, but you will need to evaluate whether members of your choir might also be prayer leaders. The risk of having prayers that might be too long or not in keeping with the truths of the faith needs to be weighed against the value of having members of the choir share their own lives of prayer. There is a benefit to seeing how each member of your choir prays; at the same time, no one should be forced to lead prayer against their will.

If you are going to offer members the opportunity to lead prayer, offer to help anyone who might want to pray but doesn't feel comfortable doing it on their own. Offer them the resources we have talked about, and offer to help them devise an appropriate collect. Whoever is going to lead prayer should normally know this ahead of time so that they can prepare this important element in the life of your choir.

Posture and Breathing

Chapter

9

Very often when I ask workshop participants, "What is the first consideration we need to make as we begin our rehearsal?" usually, the general answer is a warm up or breathing. While good breathing habits are essential to effective choral work, I believe our first consideration must be that of posture, for it is excellent posture that is foundational to achieving good breath control.

Posture

There are basically two postures that every choir singer must utilize effectively. Perhaps a gentle reminder here would help illustrate our Premise 2, "Anything (starting with posture) not under control of the individual singer is to be considered a vocal weakness, not a strength." Our job is to teach our choir members that they must think of themselves as musicians and singers, and even though they are perhaps not professionals, give them the basic tools and techniques to cultivate that skill.

1. Seated: We spend a lot of rehearsal time in a seated position. While singing I ask the choir to sit on the edge of the chair, with the rib cage held high, shoulders relaxed downward and both feet flat on the floor; no crossed legs. Ask them to sit as if their chairs had no backs, right up on the edge of their seats.

2. Standing: I always begin my rehearsals in a standing position. Many singers tend to stand in too relaxed a manner and it is important to teach them how to stand properly. Stand with your heels about six inches apart with one foot slightly ahead of the other. The rib cage should be held high, shoulders relaxed downward, and the head held erect facing forward.

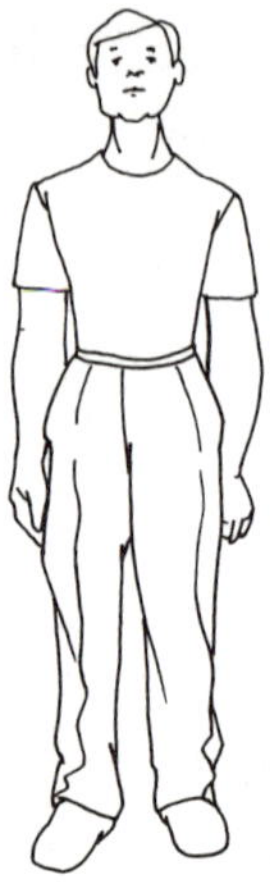

A good rule regarding posture is this: Whenever we sing, we maintain an "excellent" posture position. During non-singing time, such as the giving of verbal notes and instructions, you may relax. As soon as the next note is sounded, it is back to "excellent" posture position.

Breathing

Good breathing habits are essential to good choral singing (or any singing for that matter). My choral professor at the University of Oklahoma, Dr. Bev Henson, was fond of saying, "I don't need to teach you to breathe; God gave you the ability to breathe. I will teach you how to use your breath." That is exactly what we have to do for our singers; what is done must be done together. A lengthy explanation of the physiology of the voice with its many details is not necessary for most church choirs. Essentially all they need to be taught is how to use their diaphragm to achieve good breath support and control.

One easy way to demonstrate how to use your diaphragm is to have one of the singers lie down one the floor and place a book on his or her abdomen. It is very easy to see the book rise and fall when diaphragmatic breathing is used. Some other analogous examples to demonstrate how to use your diaphragm are the "belly laugh" and panting like a dog. These ideas are great visuals and as is often said, "one picture is worth a thousand words." If the choir begins to sound tired or sluggish, I like to ask them to check their breath support by placing the palm of their hand over the area where they can feel the diaphragm at work (at the waist near the lower ribs). Another example of proper diaphragmatic breathing is to pretend your lower abdomen is an inner tube. With your shoulders relaxed downward, take a slow breath through your nose and fill the inner tube with air. This literally "filled out" sense of the breath is a good analogy to help the group of singers feel their breath center in the trunk of the body, and greatly reinforces the concepts of good posture in singing.

Breath Control

A useful exercise that I like to do periodically during a rehearsal to refresh ourselves is rhythmic exhalation. Take a slow, deep breath through a straw without raising your shoulders or your upper chest, and release the breath on a "hiss" as you conduct to four; then repeat the exercise "hissing" to a count of eight, twelve and on the fourth repeat of the exercise, to sixteen. Used regularly, I find this technique helps each singer maintain control over his or her breath center, and develop ever greater breathing capabilities. Good breath control will also benefit the choir in tuning. If you have pitch problems, especially with the choir singing flat, stop what you are doing and work on breath control. It is at the very heart of your choral foundation.

Warm Up—Making the Sound

Chapter 10

A good warm up is essential to a good rehearsal and is especially helpful on Sunday morning, before the liturgy. You would never consider running a ten-mile race or other strenuous exercise without doing a few stretching exercises, or some deep knee bends. So it is with choral singing. Many choir directors advocate the use of stretching exercises or shoulder massage, and you might find these helpful from time to time, but I like to capture everyone's attention with things musical from the very first moment of the rehearsal. This is a good time to remember that rehearsals start on time! Our warm ups should be just that; not very long – ten minutes or less will do the job. The best choral warm ups will accomplish two goals:

1. To bring the vocal instrument to good form without stress.
2. To spark the musical imagination of the singers.

I like to see the warm up actually set the pace of the rehearsal. Ask the singers to stand, sing no louder than the person on either side and behind them, and to concentrate on listening to every voice in the room. As a choir director you probably have in mind an ideal sound you would like to hear from your choir. It does exist in your imagination and we all must work to cultivate it. Talk about the quality of that tone. Teach the choir about tone and what a good tone is. If you ask them what are the characteristics of a good tone they will usually come up with some fairly good answers, but there are three qualities of a good tone that every member should know well.

1. A good tone is relaxed, not forced or breathy, and sung with an open throat.
2. A good tone possesses some degree of intensity.
3. A good tone is sung to the center of the pitch.

Below are some warm ups that I use with regularity. They move up and down the scale in half steps.

I have included some metronome markings that may help you see the pace of the exercises.

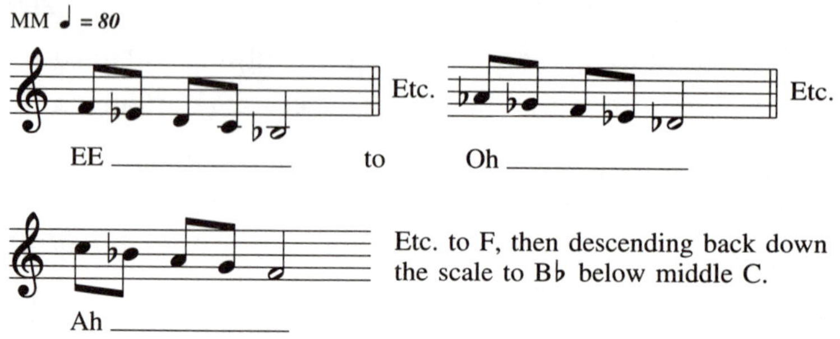

Do these quickly and insist on the best tonal production to keep the choir on its toes and monotony from setting in. No talking in between please! There are lots of warm ups that work well. Be creative and perhaps design some of your own. You can also take them from certain choral pieces that you might be working on. Be creative in your use of imagery. For instance, especially in the early part of the rehearsal, ask the singers to "place their tone" right between their eyes, on the bridge of their noses. It may help eliminate that "throaty" sound early in the process of awakening the vocal apparatus. I also like to ask them to smile a bit so as to relax the muscles around the nose and head. When all else fails, stop and do some yawning and sighing in order to lift the soft palate. More about this in the pages that follow.

Rehearsing Hymnody

Chapter 11

Hymn singing has become a standard element of the liturgy in North America. The strength of this type of music is that the strongly structured melodies are easily remembered and allow the assembly to focus more on the text being sung. The role of your choir is to help the assembly in singing hymns with which they are not familiar, to add richness to hymns by adding harmonies and other melodies to hymns that are well known, and to ensure that the assembly has the support it needs when singing unfamiliar verses of a hymn. This means that at rehearsals you should normally review all verses of a hymn. Hymns have structures, and to sing only part of a hymn can skew the message of the hymn. This is especially true of hymns that praise each person of the Trinity in turn. To leave out a verse leaves the message incomplete. Even if you have to truncate a hymn for some reason, singing all the verses in rehearsal will often bring a verse to your attention that you may not have considered using.

Knowing the structure of a hymn can help in teaching it to your choir and give them confidence as they support the song of the assembly. Two aspects of hymns are especially useful: the meter and the structure of the melody. Hymns are marked with meters that tell you how many syllables are found in each line. Knowing this will help your choir to keep the rhythm of the hymn and feel more confident in approaching the text. This also allows you to use the words of a hymn with a different, perhaps better known melody of the same meter. Most hymnals have a metrical index which lists all the hymns of a given meter.

Many hymns have a melodic structure that includes repetition of musical lines. Knowing this can speed the learning of a new hymn. For example, the hymn tune "Hymn to Joy" also known as Beethoven's "Ode to Joy" is a four-line hymn but only contains two lines of music. If we letter each line of new music, it has an AABA structure: Once you know the first line, you know the second and the last lines because they are identical.

All that remains is to learn the third line. Clearly studying the hymn in advance will make learning this hymn a very simple process indeed. When you begin to work at shaping the choral sound (see part three) this knowledge will allow you to shape lines in a complementary or contrasting manner, depending upon the nature of the text. One word of warning: Sometimes two lines will look the same at first reading, but will have one note or an ending that is different. Knowing all of this will help you lead your choir and help your assembly to sing hymns with more interest and with greater confidence.

Part THREE: Choral Sound

In my many years of experience of working with volunteer choirs, I have learned that a secure working knowledge of basic rhythm is absolutely necessary on the part of each choir member. Rhythm has to be the first consideration of any score, and you as choir director must ensure that all are familiar with basic note values and how to subdivide them to their smallest working unit of time. Other than sound itself, rhythm is the only element that is constantly present, and rhythm controls music's movement through time, influencing the life, growth, breath, and style of a score. A basic premise of choral singing is this: time is the very substance of which music is created, and our divisions or manipulations of it are the techniques by which we re-create because these manipulations can change more than any other variable. The details of rhythm therefore must be clarified each time with each piece —with everything we sing. My organ teacher taught that rhythm always came first because all the organist has to create with is time. There are no *sostenuto* or soft pedals on the organ and all articulations and phrasings must be done carefully with time. With your choir you have more flexibility of volume because each source of sound has an individual control – but this also opens up the danger of disunity in rhythm. If your choir is not united in time, they are not united in sound. If you have not taken the time to teach your choir the basics of rhythm, do so now. It may take a long time and mean that you will learn less music, but it is an investment in technique that will bless your ministry with your singers and yourself, and it will go a long way to helping your choir to sing in tune.

First, I would like you to consider rhythm and phrasing as one and to remember the basic premise of the preceding paragraph. Let's look at it another way. When you visit an art museum and see a great work of art, it is not reproduced on the spot for you at the moment of your visit by a modern painter with a set of directions. There is the painting and the one, you, who beholds the painting. The painting does not vary. It is there with all its texture, lines, shadings and all its other details. It is totally different with musical art. Throughout the work the composer gives us all sorts of notation and other symbols as a set of directions with which we try to reproduce each time what he or she heard and intended. We have, then, the composer, the performer and the listener involved in the artistic experience. Often when I hear volunteer choirs sing, I get the feeling that perhaps the composer didn't put down his or her intentions very well! It is probably more true, however, that the singers are not reading all that is necessary to recreate an accurate and exciting or moving rendition. Often a choir can "sag" or sing out of tune because the use of breath is not under rhythmic control and is not happening where and when it should. Tied notes can cause a choir to lose its place and/or the tempo to fall apart. These are all rhythmic problems; experience teaches us that it is simply not enough only to have correct pitches and rhythms. Relationships must be sought between the two, and that relationship involves rhythm and phrasing. For example, how would the choir know exactly where to take a breath, and how much time they have to do it, or how long an implied crescendo might take? The secret is learning to sing with the pulse.

Chapter 12

Rhythm and Pulse

When we talk about pulse in music, what images come to mind? The first thing I tend to think of is heartbeat. It is that underlying ebb and flow, that very heartbeat, that helps your choir to lift music off the page. It is related to the time signature, but we must not confuse metric beat with underlying pulse; they are not necessarily the same. Meter—the time signature—gives us directions for the division in time of pitch and silence symbols. It is a very important first step to negotiate in any piece, but tends in and of itself not to produce musically satisfying results. If meter refers to the duration of single notes and rests, then pulse refers to the movement of music through those single notes and rests, and also helps to define tempo. For instance, a particular piece can go no faster than the speed at which your choir can articulate/negotiate the smallest unit of time cleanly. Most choir members could tell you, I hope, that a whole note equals four quarters, but I like to teach my choir to understand that there are sixteen sixteenths, or pulses, in a whole note that we can be creative with. And so it is with all the other note values:

A WHOLE NOTE	B HALF NOTE	C QUARTER NOTE	D EIGHTH NOTE
four quarters	two quarters	two eighths	two sixteenths
eight eighths	four eighths	four sixteenths	
sixteen sixteenths	eight sixteenths		
𝅝	𝅗𝅥	♩	♪

An investment of time to teach this concept to your choir and make sure that everyone understands the principle is absolutely essential if our ensembles are to sing with a sure rhythmic footing and become familiar with how pulse works in music, especially choral singing. The other advantage of learning to sing with the pulse is that it helps your choir to maintain a good sense of tuning. Breath has to be very much in rhythmic control in order to obtain notes that are on pitch. A good exercise to demonstrate singing with the pulse is to take a simple refrain (Taizé's "Eat This Bread" is a great example) and sing the refrain in parts, but instead of singing the words sing, "oo(as in the word zoo)/da." The relationship of strong and weak pulses becomes very clear to everyone after a time or two, and all of a sudden the breath is in exactly the right place, and the refrain has a life of its own! Now we have something, a beautiful refrain, which we can begin to shape musically into phrases. And we have a little better understanding of rhythmic ensemble and what a difference it can make to the listener. Finally, as you teach your singers about rhythm, make them aware that all music moves in twos and threes; this is a basic musical fact, and this movement will produce strong/weak relationships. For example, in 4/4 time there are two groups of two, alternating strong and weak. In 3/4 time the first beat is strong, but it is still a group of three. All music will do this at all times. Your eye may see 5/4 as a time signature, but your ear will hear groups of two plus three or three plus two.

Note that there are particular rhythmic demands for chant music. Consult a chant text and talk with someone who has experience in directing chant before you attempt a chant piece for the first time, but understanding the groupings of twos and threes will get you on the right track.

Chapter 13

Rhythmic Phrases

Consider the shape of a basic musical phrase:

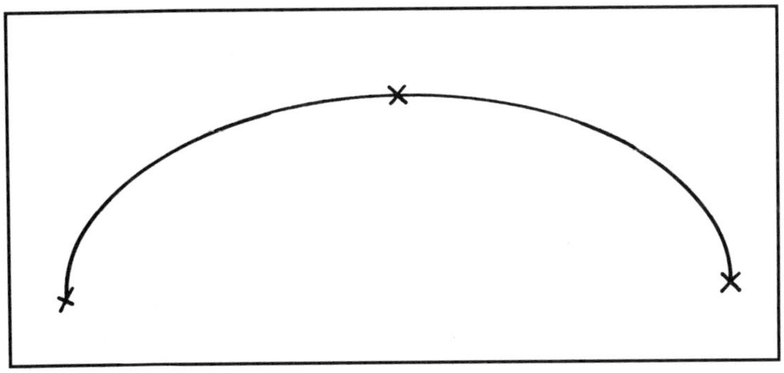

The x marks the beginning, climax or high point, and ending. When the phrase begins, it is under the pull of the climax and tension must be achieved if it is to have direction. The climax is the goal and, more importantly, the release of tension, followed by relaxation to the end of the phrase. The two sides must balance each other, and either is meaningless without that balance. The goal here is to sing with the pulse while phrasing.

Consider these examples:
Some choirs move toward the climax like this:

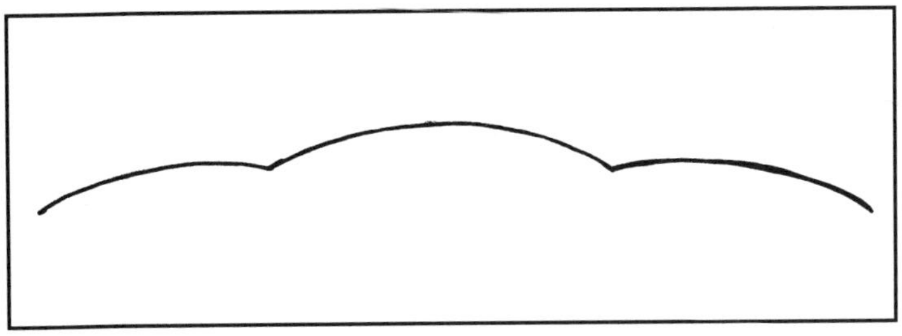

Some choirs sing only with pulse:

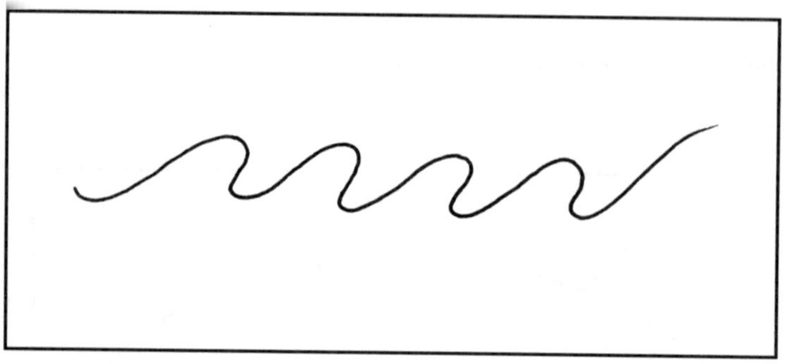

Better choirs move toward and away from the climax within the musical pulse:

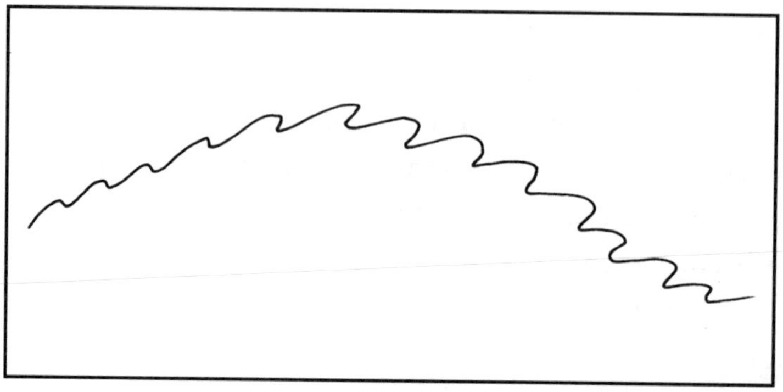

Once we are singing with the pulse another relationship to consider is dynamics. If music is a matter of proportion in all things, then dynamic changes need to occur with the pulse, not with the change of pitch. When your choir sings louder or softer because of pitch change very soon it becomes very uninteresting. For instance, consider the quarter note. If there is a crescendo indication with it, the length of that crescendo is determined by either two eighth notes, or more interestingly, four sixteenth notes. We are shaping our dynamics with the pulse of the quarter note. Imagine the possibilities that are created when we apply the pulse principle to all the different note values in a given piece. Even if there is no crescendo indicated, when we have to sing a whole note, especially in a slow tempo, it can cause a piece to wither quickly if it is approached as a single sound. The reason for this is usually because our singers are not singing the pulses of the whole note.

There is an implied crescendo or decrescendo that must be articulated because the note must be going somewhere, either toward or away from the climax. An instance where this technique is particularly useful is the tied note over the bar. Many choirs fall apart here because if we're not singing with the pulse and doing the mini-crescendo or decrescendo over the length of the tie, we lose where beat one is and the piece can crash! In music of any kind we must always know where beat one is (a good example is John Schiavone's motet, "We Adore You, O Christ") or our music-making can become erratic and careless sounding. Spending much time to help your choir develop a strong rhythmic capability will pay great dividends. Not only will they sound better, but they will be able to sing with a sense of confidence that can get them through many tough spots when it comes to live performance. It will help them achieve that life-giving, vital sound that so often shapes our moments of prayer at worship, whether it be thrilling praise or quiet reflection.

I have written a lot about how the choir can make music come alive by addressing the challenges of each note and the relationship of each note to the whole. The possibilities multiply when we approach part singing, where directors have the opportunity to shape more than one note at the same time. But in the end, how all the notes relate together is the director's artistry, it is the director's ministry. I know from experience that a solid rhythmic grounding will help choir directors discover that and will help them lead their choir into making a true ensemble sound. What is done must be done together.

Diction Skills

Chapter 14

Teaching good diction skills and habits is as important as teaching notes, rhythms, or any other choral technique. Without good diction skills we simply fail to communicate to our listeners and the message is lost. This is especially true as we try to communicate the sacred scriptures and other meaningful texts in song. What follows are some general guidelines that you might find useful. There are many fine books on choral conducting available today that treat this subject in much greater depth than is possible in this format, and these can become a valuable reference to you as a choir director. I particularly recommend Robert L. Garretson's *Conducting Choral Music.*

Choir directors must first learn to listen, and often that is hard to accomplish. We must study the texts and create mental images of what a passage should sound like and compare that with what we hear. A tape recorder can be an invaluable help with this. Very often choir directors think they have to sing with the choir, but that should only be on an infrequent basis even if you only have a choir of three or four. If that is the case, stop and ask yourself if the repertoire of the moment is too difficult to be sung without you. In any case, don't sing with the choir! Singing blocks a director's ability to hear.

As you begin to prepare your scores, analyze the text the choir will sing. That means going through every line of every part. Sort out the vowels and consonants and do some trouble-shooting. Very often if you speak the text slowly yourself, a multitude of potential diction problems will begin to surface. Some problems arise from trying to align vowel sounds with the rhythm, from diphthongs (two vowel sounds together), and some problems can arise from the way consonants are begun, especially, how they are ended. As you read the score, circle these potential problem spots and find the best way to correct them with your singers. Very often it may be a simple adjustment, but in many cases that will not be true, and we have to find a way to teach the correct solution.

Vowels

Creating and singing uniform vowel sounds is a must for every choir, but there are some pitfalls that we must address in the very beginning. For instance, did you know that words can sometime distort the rhythm of a piece? As important as singing beautiful vowels is, we have to know the when and where of singing those vowels. One way to accomplish this is to ask the choir not to just sing the words, but to sing the sounds in the words. As a small example, consider the opening line of the hymn, "O God Our Help In Ages Past." Many choirs often sing the word "our" as two eighth notes instead of just a quarter as it is written. The result is an unconscious change in the rhythm of the word. It must be treated as a diphthong. Diphthongs consist of two vowel sounds within one syllable. The general rule is that we sing the sustained vowel as long as possible and add the vanishing vowel as if it were a consonant; this should be done rhythmically. If the "vanishing" precedes the sustained vowel, as in the word "you," it must be sung slightly ahead of the beat. The point is that choir directors must make the necessary adjustments so that their words do not change or distort the rhythm of a particular piece. Think rhythmic diction. There are six diphthongs in the English language that we need to consider carefully. The rhythm of these sounds must be carefully decided on by the director and passed on to the choir. It is important that you speak these diphthongs slowly in score study so that their content becomes very clear.

Illustrative Symbol	Examples
AH + EE	Night
AH + short OO	Now
AW + IH	Voice
AY + IH	They
OH + short OO	So
IH + short OO	New

When negotiating diphthongs, in these examples, the rhythmic value of the note must change so that the first vowel carries the word's primary sound.

Example	Note Value	Sung As
Night	Quarter	Dotted Eighth+Sixteenth
Now	Half	Dotted Quarter+Eighth

Recall that some words begin with two vowel sounds with the second sound carrying the word's primary sound. In this case, the first vowel sound must be sung ahead of the beat. Some good examples are: you, yes, where, we. Words that begin with Y are an EE (long E) sound. Words that begin with W are an OO (short as in who) sound.

Consonants

If beautifully negotiated vowel sounds carry the bulk of our choral sound, then consonants provide clarity and articulation. One way to explore the consonant content of a piece is to whisper the text loudly. If you lower the volume of the vowels, the consonant sounds appear to be much louder and problems are easily spotted. The general rule is that consonant sounds must be in direct proportion to the vowel sound. There is nothing more pedestrian than hearing a choir sing a beautiful sound that is ruined by too loud a consonant, so great care must be given to these sounds.

If a final consonant is followed by a rest, then that consonant sound should be placed on the rest so that we sing the full value of the note with pitched sound. However, when there are no rests, for instance in the middle of a phrase, we must create them by rhythmically negotiating the pitchless sound and making sure everyone marks their scores the same way. At times words can begin with two consonants. The first is usually non-pitched and the second pitched as in the words "crown" or "please." The first consonant is negotiated slightly ahead of the beat and the second is placed on the beat. Remember, these are general rules. Let us examine some other categories of consonants.

- Voiced (have pitch), sung deeply ahead of the beat
    - M-Mary, N-new, L-love
- Voiced explosive(carry sound but not pitch)
    - B-baby, G-God, D-day
- Purely explosive(initiated with air)
    - P-people, T-tell, K-keep
- Sibilants (include hissing sound)
    - S-so, F-far, SH-shine
- Aspirate
    - H-how

Some other tips that are helpful regarding consonants are:

S—To avoid hissing like snakes on the end of a word, make this sound as short as possible. Remember that music is a matter of proportion in all things. A final S or T that is too loud may be fixed by asking the singers as a group to sing the final consonant but to immediately open their mouths wide up after doing so. They will hear it shorter.

R—The American "r" is a real problem and one that many singers tend to sing as long as possible. It is instinct. Again, when it occurs in the middle or at the end of a word, make it as short as possible and add it at the last second. When it occurs at the beginning of a word, flip or roll it.

"Eliding"—Sometimes it is desirable to connect the consonants. First, decide how *legato* the line should be. If the words need to be more articulated, then separate the two with a rhythmic space in between. Have the choir speak the two sounds before singing them. Demonstrate what you wish the choir to do.

It takes some time to become really good at word-problem-solving but it is a fascinating study in itself. But, like any good sleuth, we can find all the clues in the score if we take the necessary time, as directors, to filter through all those details. Good choir directors must develop a love for the English language. It is a life-long study.

Making the Ensemble Sound

Chapter 15

Good singers practice good habits in the physical sense but often need to be reminded to practice the habit of good listening. This is where choir directors should begin shaping the sound of the their choirs. It is not easy always to use your ears while performing your own task, but it is a goal to work on constantly. Not only is it important for us to listen, but we must know what to listen for. For instance, the most important concept to teach in the beginning is that the choir should sing with a vertical rather that a horizontal attitude of the jaw and mouth. An expression I like to use is to make the sound "stand up." This is especially helpful when working on good vowel sounds. Another concept I like to start the choir year with is listening to breathing and breathing rhythmically with those around you. I cannot stress enough the importance of developing a good rhythmic sense. It will save your life! I'd much rather hear the wrong note sung at the right time than all the right notes sung at the wrong time.

Vowels

The pivotal point of making a beautiful choral sound is the choir's understanding of proper vowel formation. Beautifully formed and sung vowels are important because they carry the bulk of our sound. This idea is particularly important in today's church choirs because of the tremendous diversity of cultures found in most parishes. No only do we have national accents to deal with, but the wide range of regional accents makes good vowel formation essential in creating a homogenous ensemble sound. Even after thirteen years with my own choir, we still have the "vowel of the month" to work on at every rehearsal. Let's look at it another way. If you were to ask twenty people to read the same newspaper article out loud, you would hear twenty different regional or national accents. That is fine for reading, but that effort in choral singing would create a train wreck! This is a great example of WHAT IS DONE MUST BE DONE TOGETHER. We have to shape our vowels the same way, in the same place, at the same time so that we at least have a hope of creating a blended ensemble. It is the first step, and I recommend that you take one vowel a month and have everyone make a concerted effort to sing that vowel the very same way, listening critically to one another. I like to experiment with the sounds by asking the choir to first sing their vowels lying down (a horizontal attitude) and then sing the same vowels standing up.

Tone

Another very important concept that we must teach our choirs is the use of head tone. This is that wonderful sound that happens when the soft palate of the throat is lifted and the nasal/pharyngeal cavities of the head open up, vitally affecting the tone.

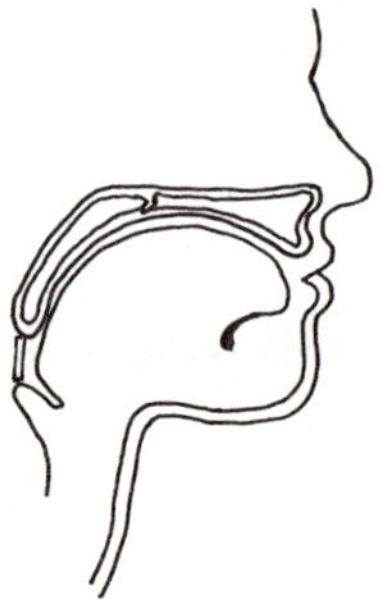

In teaching the choir how to lift the soft palate there are some surefire things to help clarify this technique. First, ask the singers to take a very quick breath, and it must be quick, as if someone scared or surprised them suddenly from behind. They should feel a definite cooling sensation in the back of their throats. Try this several times until everyone feels it. That is where your soft palate is located. Another easy technique to feel the lifting is to have everyone yawn and sigh. You cannot help but feel the lift just as if you opened a tiny umbrella in your mouth. A word of caution is appropriate here: I have heard many choir directors use the phrase "drop your jaw" in an effort to produce an open resonant sound. While a relaxed, flexible jaw is desirable, that constant idea of pulling downward can become a great source of tension for the singer and is much less important than the inner expansion of the nose, throat and pharynx areas.

Here is an exercise I like to use, sometimes as an additional warm-up at rehearsal, designed to demonstrate how lifting of the soft palate affects our vowel sound.

1. Begin on F above middle C and sing the word "hung," asking the singers to go right to the NG sound in the word.
2. On a very slow count to five, change the sound ever so gradually to AH.
3. Sing five notes descending to B flat, keeping the lifted position, using the Vowels AH-OH-AH-OH-AH.

and so on ascending

Now translate this concept to music. Sing something simple like Taizé's " Eat This Bread," first with a hum. When you hum, sing with your teeth apart but your lips closed and retain the lifted position in the mouth. Now try just your ordinary, garden variety, "driving in the car" hum. It sounds so flat and uninteresting in comparison. The reason is that in the correct hum the nasal and pharyngeal cavities were open, usually causing the mask of the face to vibrate or tingle. This is a good thing! It is called head tone, and it is that blessed sound we all love and hope for our choirs to use. Practice this over and over again until it simply becomes automatic. It may take several weeks or months to form the habit, but it is well worth the effort.

Blend

The next step to consider is creating a blend so that we have an effective way of integrating individual voices into the ensemble. "Blend" in choral music is the way different sections of your choir sing together to create one music. For most choir directors the concept of blend and how to achieve it remains cloudy, but it goes hand in hand with proper resonation and good vowel formation. The human voice is probably the most expressive and sensitive of musical instruments and has virtually unlimited possibilities for shading and color. Our task is to find ways to explore those attributes while allowing for individual differences of timbre. This should be very exciting to the creative choir director. Just for a moment, think of what an orchestral score looks like. The composer has already done a lot for us by providing shading and color through the use of dynamics and instrumentation. Oftentimes choir directors are left to their own devices of choral orchestration and we have to decide what the tone of the choir should be for any given piece. Remember—be flexible when teaching tone or blend. This means studying our scores and becoming familiar with periods and styles of repertoire because we don't necessarily want to use one single type of tone for every piece. That would be like using a Bach orchestra to sing a Brahms requiem! This is where our knowledge of musical styles comes into play. For instance, the rich voluptuous sound of a piece from the Romantic period may not be appropriate for the more restrained, controlled sound of the Baroque period.

There are many ways to achieve a good sense of blend, but here is one that I like to use in general, and is a way to start.

1. Choose a short, simple musical selection in four-part homophonic style. Taize's "Eat This Bread" or a chorale will work perfectly. The choir should not have to struggle with reading

and a simple rhythm and fairly comfortable range (not too high for the altos and not too low for the tenors) is important.

2. Begin with the altos, especially if they are a strong section. Have them sing the first phrase using a soft vowel texture such as "poo" as in Winnie the.
3. Next have the tenors sing the alto part in their own octave with the altos, asking the altos to listen to the tenors as they sing and try to lose their sound into the sound of the tenors. This will produce a brighter sound in the alto section when they are singing with tenors and tends to prevent the tendency to become too dark and "hooty" when they tone match with each other.
4. Now invert the procedure by having the tenors sing their own line and have the altos sing the same line with the tenors. Have the tenors try to match the alto quality. This has the same effect in inversion that step three achieved for the altos and helps the tenors to avoid sounding strident.
5. The next step is to have the altos sing the tenor line and the tenors sing the alto line simultaneously, listening for tonal blend. Then ask them to sing their own parts while maintaining that sense of blend. This exercise so far suggests that blend is a matter of tone color and shows that it is possible to blend voices on different pitches as well as unison singing. The key is listening.
6. We have locked the tone or blend from the inside out, and so now we add the soprano line. If they have been listening carefully to the exercise, their ears will already have a vision of the basic tone. Since soprano tone does not

actually blend with alto and tenor tone, ask them to listen and simply use a quality that is compatible with what we have instead of trying to lose their voices in the blend.

7. Now we have a fairly good triadic blend, and we simply add the bass line with great care, making sure that it supports the other voice, adding new harmonies where called for, but never dominating the sound.

These are ideas that have worked well for me over the years but they are not one-time fixes. For a concept to become clearly understood, you must be use it over and over again so that it becomes part of your singers' habits.

Vibrato

Speaking of good habits, one of the most problematic aspects of good ensemble singing is the use of vocal vibrato. I am not addressing the use of vibrato in solo singing, but in choral singing. Every director has her or his own concept of what constitutes an appropriate amount of vibrato and at what point vibrato begins to destroy the choral blend. Some directors say yes to vibrato, and some say absolutely not when it comes to ensemble singing. It is both a matter of taste and a common dilemma for most of us. What is more, some genres of music call for more or less vibrato: Rennaisance era polyphony, for example, calls for very little vibrato, while some contemporary styles call for more vibrato. Even with the style of music to guide us, there is no single correct answer, but some general observations are in order here to help you establish your own guidelines. There are many underlying reasons for considering the use of vibrato; the most important is accuracy of pitch. Singers must use their ears carefully in vibrato control in order to sing a passage in tune and on pitch. Too much vibrato can produce a pitch that is a half step high or a half step low. We agreed that a good tone is always sung to the center of the pitch and involves critical listening by the individual. In other words, there is a limit to how wide or fast a vibrato can be and still maintain the identity of a given pitch. If in a given passage the choir sounds flat, stop and examine the amount of vibrato being used. For example, your choir may be singing a passage in the tonality of F Major; the sopranos are singing F, but their vibrato includes E, the leading tone! The tenors may be singing C but their vibrato includes a B Natural, not even in the key. Once you show your singers what they are doing to the harmony, the singers can still use vibrato, but must make the simple adjustment of not sounding these notes that pull the pitch downward, sounding flat. Remember that music is a matter of proportion in all things and a vibrato in choral singing cannot be wider or slower than the size and depth of tone and still be in good taste. Directors, as well as singers, usually think they are hearing what they see on the printed page. This aural illusion can be broken by listening to the choir often without looking at the score. Only then do we hear what our listeners hear. These aspects, the shaping of vowels and tone and the use of blend and vibrato, are tools in your kit to ensure that singers work together to make the most of their individual talents and your abilities as director. When everyone is pulling in the same direction and working at building up the same good habits, beautiful things can happen. True choral sound is a beautiful thing.

Gesture Technique and Basic Conducting

Chapter 16

The use of gesture in leading the choir is an important tool for every choir director to acquire. The basic gestures of conducting are easy to learn and, given enough practice over time, will become second nature. Experience is the best teacher.

Perhaps the first step toward developing a good gesture technique, and it takes time, is to develop an excellent personal sense of rhythm. The ability to establish a tempo and maintain it through time is essential and must be practiced regularly. Only then can we communicate through arm movement and hand signals what is required for the choir to render a piece of music well. Conducting is a matter of personal and creative expression, not rocket science, and is an exciting experience when we learn to translate our musical ideas through movement and gesture.

Learning to conduct the basic patterns of two, three and four is simple and should be the first order of business, as many pieces use these time signatures. Consider the pattern of 4/4 time. Imagine a square box or room in front of your upper body. Place your right arm at a comfortable distance, about shoulder height and move through the pattern, thinking floor-wall-wall-ceiling in a recurring motion to get the feel of the pattern. Don't worry about an exact gesture if you are just learning, but rather concentrate on becoming at ease with your arm motions while maintaining a moderate tempo. Any awkwardness will disappear as your familiarity increases and a sense of fluidness should characterize your motions.

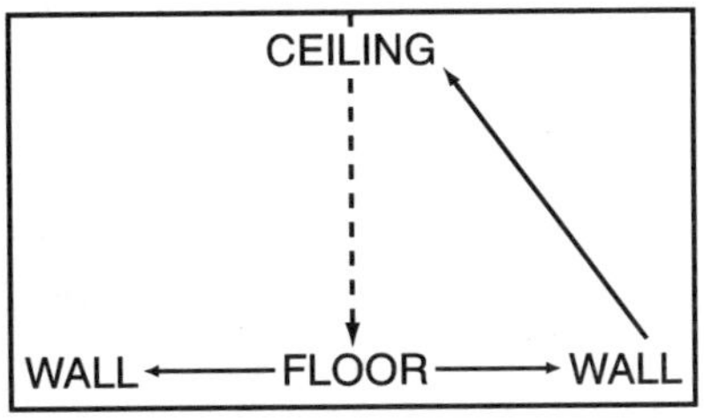

Now practice "placing" your beats, like dribbling a basketball slowly, on a steady count of four, not fast and not slow. Do the same practice for a time signature of three and also for two.

3 Pattern

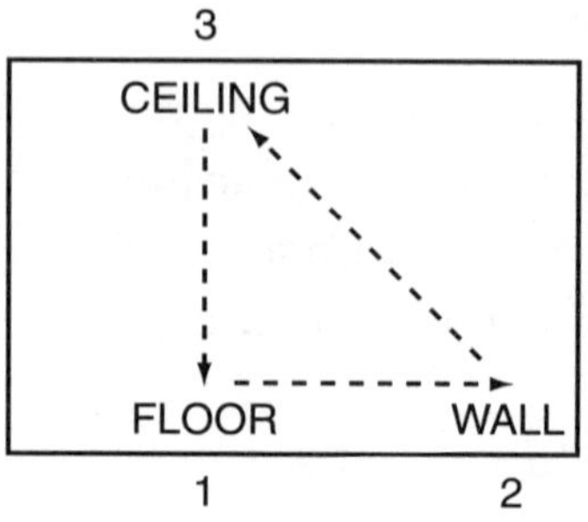

2 Pattern

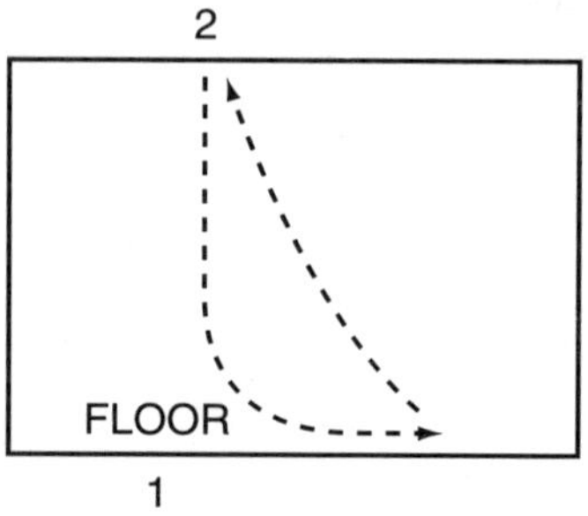

It can be very helpful to practice this in front of a mirror. Use the dimensions of a music stand desk to establish your conducting plane, the area where your patterns will occur. Work to place beat one in the same spot each time. The size of the gesture should not be too large or too small and will always relate to the dynamic being sung; smaller gestures for piano (soft) and mezzo piano, medium ones for mezzo forte, and larger ones still for forte.

Establish your gesture and tempo by always giving a clear preparatory beat. It tells the choir when and how long to breathe to make an entrance. The preparatory beat also gets your pattern going and is determined by the tempo of the piece. If the piece begins on beat one, the prep happens on beat four. If the piece begins with beat four, the prep happens on beat three and so on. These preparatory beats are important because they tell the choir the "when" (how long) and "where" (which beat) to breathe, establishing a good sense of tempo. After a bit of practice it becomes just as easy to cue with the left hand while maintaining the beat with your right hand. A cut-off can work in the same way if needed during the course of a piece, but it is important to pinpoint the exact and rhythmic "where" that the cue will happen. This is a vital part of score preparation and it is necessary to practice these ahead of time. If your first efforts at gesture technique seem discouraging, don't give up. Practice is the name of the game! A good gesture technique takes time to develop in order to achieve a certain degree of consistency and it is possible for most choir directors to master.

Pieces with a time signature of six, such as 6/8, require a bit of special attention and the gesture used will always be determined by the tempos indicated in the score. Remember, if there is no tempo indication, your can establish one by this method. Sing each line to yourself and note the smallest unit of time, usually an eighth or sixteenth note. The tempo can never be faster than the smallest unit of time can be sung cleanly. If a piece, say in 6/8 time, is in a moderate or faster tempo, it is best to conduct it using a pattern of two. If the tempo is slow or very slow, it is best to conduct the piece giving each beat clearly. The pattern looks like this.

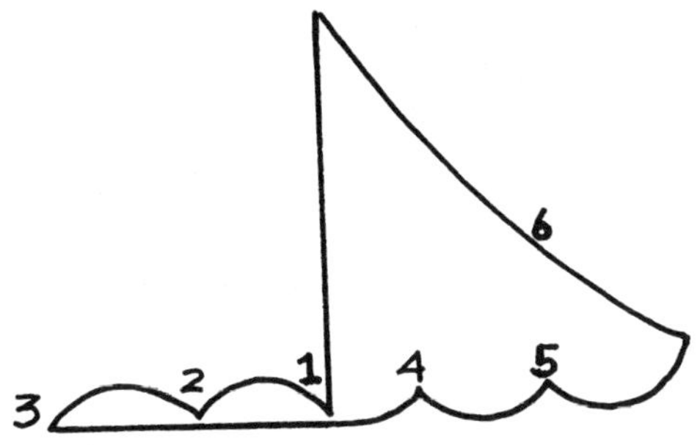

As this pattern is sometime difficult to control, practice it often with the use of voices or instruments, and use the mirror.

Often a piece will utilize a slow tempo in 3/4 or 4/4 and it becomes necessary to conduct it with a sub-divided beat pattern. This can be achieved by slightly bouncing or pulsing each beat twice of the pattern being used. The ability to effectively conduct a sub-divided pattern is especially important when working with a group of instruments in order to maintain a steady beat in the slow tempo. Take special care to always place beat one in the same way each time. If a piece is in 5/4 or perhaps 7/8, the respective patterns used will become three plus two or two plus three and four plus three or three plus four depending on how the text and phrases need to be rendered.

These and many other aspects of gesture technique are inherently present in the music if we take the time to study our scores and prepare ahead of time. There is nothing more difficult to cope with than being insecure or unprepared with the details of a particular rhythmic passage in any given piece. Schedule your repertoire in such a way that you have time to make informed decisions about those details, especially problem areas. It is not only fun to uncover those clues, but your choir will greatly appreciate your efforts to help them sing better.

Conducting from the Console

Chapter 17

To my knowledge there is no definitive resource or well-known book on the subject of conducting from the console. It is a tradition that has been verbally handed down through many years and can be a rewarding and satisfying experience for those who are called to that particular discipline. I use the term "called" because as an organist-conductor, you must want to do both skills to become good at it. It is not a compromise to standing and directing, but rather a different way of expressing musical matters of performance that every choir director must attend to. It is also an increasingly popular position in parishes where budget restraints prevent appropriate salaries for a separate director and organist. It requires the mastering of two disciplines to become a successful organist-director, and honoring those skills can be frustrating if one has to struggle with either basic conducting or a solid foundation in organ playing. What follows are some general observations based on personal experience over many years of playing and directing. They are presented in the form of tips which will help you hone your skills in this important ministry.

Conducting from the Console
Some General Observations

A. Develop a Well Trained Choir and Totally Responsive Choir
   1. Never accept your choir's failure to follow your direction
   2. Make a point of not always being predictable at rehearsal (to sharpen the awareness in your singers of the need to pay attention)
      - change tempos vary duration of fermatas
      - pause before an attack or entrance

3. In short, require attentiveness
   - be good humored but firm
   - do some good-natured ribbing when someone sings out of turn
   - do not embarrass anyone
4. Expect and insist on nothing less than total attention
5. Help your choir develop a good sense of confidence
   - If they think they can't they won't
   - Be consistent in your work during the liturgy
   - Make decisions about any variables or score changes early on
   - Realize that there is no such thing as being over-rehearsed
6. Have good sight lines between you and your choir
   - Rearrange the placement of the console
   - Develop a seating plan and then stick to it
   - Occasionally experiment with other arrangements of space
   - Use mirrors when needed
   - Using the photocopier, reduce the size of your music scores
   - Install a glass or Lucite music rack
   - Be conscious of what the choir hears from the organ (balance)
   - Have another person check the balance in the rest of the church

B. Improve Your Own Technique
   1. Know your music well
      - Rearrange the keyboard part as needed
      - Free up one hand as much as possible
   2. Know your basic harmony well for each given piece

- Basic chord knowledge is essential
- Learn to invert chords automatically
- Practice this skill and rewrite chords
- Don't double notes with the left hand
- Use a registration that blends with your voices
- Improve your pedal technique
    a. put three voices in the playing hand with the bass line in the pedal
- Set pistons for choir using mostly flute and string stops

3. Refine your directing technique
    - Practice your directing technique, marking when specific cues are needed
    - Refine your gestures, especially the gesture for preparation/entrance and cut off
        a. make sure that these are not exaggerated
    - Learn to use your head or hand in directing; teach your choir to follow these cues
    - Learn to pick up the directing beat at any point in the music
    - Develop a vocabulary of clear and consistent hand signals
    - Eliminate any motions that are not needed to produce a quality choral sound
    - Make good (and perhaps opt for the simpler) choices in repertoire
    - Realize that some pieces are too complicated to conduct from the bench—you might consider an alternate keyboard player in particular cases or on special days
    - Solve any difficulties at rehearsal, not at the liturgy
    - Plan time in your schedule to prepare and practice accompaniments and gestures
    - Make video recordings of your work so that you can evaluate your skills

C. Other Possibilities

1. Spend part of your rehearsal time standing to direct the choir
2. Do some a cappella work—all choirs can and should do this
3. Don't compensate by talking more—comments should be quick, direct and explicit
4. Establish good rehearsal habits, paying even more attention to the issues dealt with in part two of this book.

And always remember that conducting from the console is not about the art of the perfect, but the art of the possible, and is only as successful as your choir is prepared.

Ending and after the Rehearsal

Chapter 18

Having kept the choir rehearsal moving at a good pace, you have completed everything you wanted to do in the two hours you set aside for the rehearsal. It is generally a bad idea to go longer than two hours—our voices just can't take it—but if you need an additional ten minutes to complete some important aspect, at least ask permission of your singers before pressing on.

The end of the rehearsal should be in a simple prayer, perhaps a prayer that everyone can recite together, followed by a blessing. All Christians are able and in fact called to offer blessings to each other, and the end of a choir rehearsal is as good a place as any to accomplish this.

Once all your choir members have gone, spend a few minutes going over what happened at the rehearsal. For those items you are working on for use later than this weekend, make a few notes as to what needs to be worked on at the next rehearsal. For those pieces that you will be singing this weekend, make any notes on what will need to be gone over at the warm-up rehearsal that will happen before the liturgy.

Finally, spend a few moments examining your performance at the rehearsal. Did you get bogged down on something that was not all that important? Are you going to need new approaches for teaching a particularly stubborn passage? What is your overall opinion of how the rehearsal went? Do not rely on your memory for these details, and do not wait until the next day to write these down because you are sure to forget something important.

All of these post-rehearsal elements are designed to ensure that you get the most out of the rehearsal for yourself. It would be a shame to lose any of the insights that came from the common rehearsal. It is also singularly frustrating to your singers if you make the same mistakes over and over again. Just as your choir learns their music during the rehearsal, so too you need to learn and build on what they have done.

Part FOUR: Ritual Celebration Rituals

Now that you have held a successful choir rehearsal, all that remains is to reap the harvest of the hard work that you and your singers have done. While there will be times when things will go wrong and you will wonder if the people singing at liturgy were even at the rehearsal, these will be balanced over time by those moments when the inspiration of the moment will lead you and your choir into places that you did not expect to go. The goal of the next several chapters is to create a constant set of behaviors which will keep confusion to a minimum and lay the way open for the action of the Holy Spirit.

Sunday—Day of Resurrection, Day of Ministry

Whether your choir sings at liturgy at an anticipated celebration on Saturday evening or on Sunday morning, everything needs to be steeped in the importance of Sunday as the day of the resurrection and the day of choral ministry. Why should the day make a difference? What particular quality does this day have that affects the ministry of a choir and a choir director? It may not be something that we talk about a lot, but there is a very close relationship between Sunday and choral singing. One of the primary purposes of singing is praise of God in common. When we sing as a choir we join several voices into one. When we sing God's praises as one on Sunday we are true successors to the first disciples of Christ, whose reaction to the resurrection was to spend their lives praising God in the temple (see Luke 24: 52–53). Since the resurrection happened on Sunday, choirs who lead singing on that day (or at the anticipated liturgy on Saturday evening) are proclaiming the joy of the resurrection once again. It is a form of anamnesis, or making powerful memory; it is our particular way of participating in the power of the resurrection of Christ.

Preparations before the Warm-up Rehearsal

Chapter 19

In general a choir director needs to be in the building at least half an hour before the time the liturgy is scheduled to begin. No matter how prepared you are, there are a number of elements that can only be confirmed in this last half hour. If it should happen that you are not well organized, you may need as much as an hour to prepare for the celebration.

You need to develop a set of steps that you follow every time you direct your choir. The same should be true of your choir members. The order of service should include the following:

Prayer. First things first—spend a few moments in prayer, quietly placing all that you will do this day in the hands of the one who has given you the ability and opportunity to be a choir director. This time need not be structured, but it is an important tool in keeping the accent on the service aspect of your work.

Checking your music. Of course you had prepared your music for the rehearsal and had noted any particular difficulties that needed to be reviewed before the liturgy, but it is still a good practice to make sure that you have everything that you need in the proper order.

Meeting with the presiding minister or master of ceremonies. Again, the assumption is that you have been in regular communication with those who prepare the liturgy in your parish, but it is still important to meet for a moment with the presiding minister. All too often things come up at the last minute, and so a quick rundown of how you understand the liturgy is going to unfold will give the presiding minister or the master of ceremonies (a person who the presiding minister relies on to attend to all the details of the ceremony) an opportunity to tell you of any changes that might have been made. It is also an opportunity to greet the presiding minister and offer any musical assistance that might be needed. I have known priests who would, from time to time, want to sing the preface; this meeting time would be the opportunity for them to tell me this and then I would in turn suggest singing the preface dialogue. Knowing this, I could prepare the choir to support the singing of the peoples' responses in the dialogue. Without this meeting the singers would have been caught unprepared.

The Warm-up Rehearsal to the Beginning of the Celebration

Chapter

20

At some point not less than fifteen minutes before the beginning of the liturgy you should assemble the choir for their warm-up rehearsal. If it is important that normal rehearsals not drag, it is crucial that this brief rehearsal be focused and fast-paced. The rehearsal should happen in the choir room, not in the worship space, since there are people there preparing for the liturgy. The rehearsal immediately before the liturgy needs to have a stronger structure to it. If you do the same things in the same order every week, your singers and instrumentalists will be better able to keep pace. Here is one suggested order.

Warm-up. If you minister on Sunday morning, warming up the voices of your singers is even more important than at the end of the day. While some of the same exercises used in chapter 9 might be useful, time will not permit a full range of warm-up exercises. Gently singing over one of the hymns for the liturgy is a way to awaken the voices while at the same time preparing the music that will actually be used in the liturgy.

Talking through issues. Once the voices of your choir are ready, talk about the important issues that you made note of at the end of the rehearsal. Keep these limited in number and be as clear as possible as to your expectations.

Singing the tough spots. Sing through not more than one or two difficult passages to ensure that your singers will have heard them one last time and have the correct notes in their mind as close as possible to the time when they will be called upon to sing them.

Finally, end with a brief prayer. Here a set prayer makes the most sense. It can be a verse—perhaps the doxology by Thomas Ken set to the Old Hundredth hymn tune, "Praise God from whom all blessings flow," or some short acclamation that fits your choir's temperament. The goal is to move your ministry into a more structured behavior as we all enter into the more structured environment of the liturgy.

Once this prayer is completed there needs to be no further explanations to your choir; they simply move to their places and prepare themselves to sing. They should be in place no more than five minutes before the scheduled start time so as not to become restless, but also should be present not less than two minutes before the start time. Clearly synchronization of your watch with the sacristy clock is a very important detail.

Chapter 21

The Choir Director During the Celebration

Choir directors are called upon to fill as many as three different roles during the liturgical celebration. Many choir directors I have spoken to over the years find it difficult to do all three all the time, but it is important to work at making all of them at least a part of what you do at each liturgy.

The choir director as member of the people of God. This is perhaps the most difficult aspect of your ministry as choir director during the liturgy. No matter how complicated things get, no matter what else is going on, you are to be a model for the choir and for the assembly on how to participate in liturgical prayer. You should hear the readings rather than spending your time turning pages and trying to look ahead in the celebration. You should participate in peoples' responses and other elements of their role in the liturgy. In short, you should be praying the celebration with the people.

The choir director's ministry of leadership. As director, it is your goal to lead the choir in their ministry, inspiring confidence in your singers so that when you make a gesture they will respond without reserve. Your goal is to make the work of your choir and instrumentalists an act of prayer. If the singers are worried about the technical details of their work, it is much more difficult for them to enter into the ministerial and prayer aspects of what they are doing. Choirs that have strong leaders are better able to pray the words they sing, and choirs that pray together as they sing have a distinct advantage: they are already of one mind and heart.

The choir director as liturgical expert. As choir director you are one of a small number of people who are looked to for leadership during the liturgy. Once the liturgy has begun, you may be the one to work out the problems, large or small, which occur during the celebration. The presiding minister is in a sense unable to address such issues from the area around the altar, so you can expect other ministers to look to you for answers if something goes awry. This means that you need to be constantly in tune with what comes next and who is responsible for what in the liturgical celebration. You can give the look to the lector who has missed a cue; you can signal to the ushers to go and help the person who has fainted during the Mass; but you can only do so if you know exactly where we are in the liturgy and what comes next.

The balance between these tasks is not always easy to maintain, but if you consistently attend to the demands of all of these areas I believe that over time both you and your choir will feel more a part of the assembly's prayer and that you will be viewed more a part of the leadership of the parish.

Debriefing

Chapter 22

Because you have planned out each liturgical celebration on a separate sheet, once the liturgy is over you have a golden opportunity to record in writing what areas worked especially well, what areas still need attention and what should never be done again. Marking over your planning sheets with simple comments will take only a few moments but will provide you with a valuable planning guide for the following year. Imagine having several years of planning guides at your disposal—some ideas that worked once do not bear the test of time and will gradually be marked as something to be discarded; others will be perennially popular. Only record-keeping will give you the facts you need for future planning.

In a separate and private place, write down any comments you need to make about your own performance as director, and that of your instrumentalists and singers. These are notes for you and only you. But if over time that alto or tenor consistently nods off or appears not to be paying attention, repeated notes to this effect in your book will give you the information you need to approach your singer with the problem and propose a workable solution. If the time comes that a member, even a volunteer member, of your choir needs to be fired, this information will be crucial. Good news also needs to be recorded so that you can offer public praise to the soprano or bass section for getting that very difficult part. You need to write this down because you will forget to mention it by the time the next rehearsal comes around.

The goal of this few moments after the liturgy is to keep your choir moving forward. The goal is to ensure that each member and you, as leader keep moving forward. If there is no record kept of how things are succeeding or failing, there is no easy way to see the way to an ever stronger ministry and ever more beautiful music.

Part FIVE: Administer and Minister

The work of the choir director is a ministry of administration. You do not make a sound, but rather cause the sound to be made. You are not the singer, you are the one who ensures that those who come to sing can do so in a way that is aesthetically pleasing while still a true act of prayer. All of this means that you will invest a good deal of time in evaluating what you have, making choices for the group and helping the entire assembly enter more deeply into the prayer of the liturgy. The following chapters are designed to help make you conscious of the effects that result from the choices you make.

Chapter 23

Selecting Music

This is an awesome job for any choir director, but it can be fun and satisfying. Our first responsibility is to provide music for the assembly. That includes hymns/songs, psalms, Mass settings, and a variety of pieces to support and enhance the rites of the church. This will involve a collaboration with the liturgical ministers of the parish. While you are the one qualified to make selections, the liturgy director does have a role (in collaboration with you and the pastoral leadership of the parish) in laying out how the rites will unfold and the desired mood called for by the moment. How this collaboration unfolds varies widely from place to place, with some having no collaboration at all to others where everybody picks everything together. The principle of subsidiarity should apply to liturgical and musical choices as much as it does to the other aspects of church life. The decision should be made by the person furthest down on the chain of command who is competent to make that decision. There will be times when pastors or even bishops will make more or less insistent requests, but you should strive to ensure that within the constraints of the liturgy you are responsible for making the selections of which piece of music will be used at a given moment.

Many of our assemblies have been deluged with new songs and other compositions, and in some ways, we have taught them always to expect something new. It is time for us to think a little less about what is new, and spend more time thinking about what works well, or wears well, when it comes to liturgical music. There is a constant stream of newly published music that is exciting, but "new" doesn't always mean "better." The time has come for us to look at our music selections with as much care as we choose the very food we put in our bodies. If we eat nothing but junk food, we will have junky bodies! And if we are what we eat, then perhaps we are what we sing. What we need now is not so much more music, but music that is solidly and exquisitely crafted. Ask yourself the question, "Does this composition have that timeless, precious quality that marks it as truly good art and worthy of the sacred? Is there skill in this writing?" In order to do this on our own, we need to know about music theory, compositional techniques, and music literature. We have to know about Bach cantatas and imitative technique, because without an understanding of the music we use, we cannot develop the ability to make good judgments about new music! If you do not have a background that allows you to make this musical judgement easily, then consult with people who do. And, speaking of judgments, every music director should have a working knowledge of the documents *Music in Catholic Worship* and *Liturgical Music Today.* (These two documents are available in booklet form from Oregon Catholic Press under the English title *The Music Documents* (OCP 10178 PQ) and in Spanish under the title *Documentos* (OCP 11202 PQ).) The directives for selecting repertoire are very clearly laid out in these documents under three judgments:

The musical judgment: Knowledge about the skill of composition and what constitutes a well-crafted and solid piece of music is absolutely necessary.

The liturgical judgment: What kind of music is called for at particular moments of the rite? Our task is to help proclaim the word and certain pieces can become a distraction to proclamation.

The pastoral judgment: Does a particular piece of music help the assembly to pray in song? Does it express our faith in this moment, in this place, or in this culture? Sometimes a certain composition may be wonderful music but not necessarily appropriate to a particular celebration.

Of course, all of these principles are important, but we need to do more; we must become students of the scriptures. Only through this endeavor will we come to know deeply the stories around which we are planning music. Planning guides are available from all the Catholic publishers and are most helpful, but nothing takes the place of knowing the scripture readings in depth. The basic plan for the liturgical year chooses readings for the Sunday celebrations on a three-year cycle, focusing on the gospel of Matthew in year A, Mark (and the bread of life discourse from the gospel of John) in year B and Luke in year C. The first reading is generally, but not always chosen in light of the gospel reading, and the psalm is chosen in the light of the first reading. The second reading is chosen according to a different pattern. If you are not familiar with the liturgical year and the scriptures chosen for these celebrations you really need to do some serious study in this area. Knowing how the readings are chosen and how the liturgical year unfolds will make many of your tasks as choir director much easier. Certainly choosing music becomes much more manageable, but so too does explaining why you are teaching your choir a specific piece of music.

Another important resource for selecting music is the NPM (National Association of Pastoral Musicians) Director of Music Ministries Division's, "Lectionary Choral Anthem Project." Its purpose is to list repertoire suggestions, independent of publishing industry interests, for parish choir directors. Those responsible for selecting and preparing choral anthems will find a rich storehouse of suggestions from which to choose choral music related to the Sunday scriptures. In addition, we should be on the mailing lists of all the major publishers, Catholic and non-Catholic, so that we are aware of what is available.

Oregon Catholic Press
P.O. Box 18030
Portland, OR 97218-0030
1800 LITURGY (548-8749)
http://www.ocp.org

GIA
7404 South Mason Avenue
Chicago, IL 60638
(800) GIA-1358 (442-1358)
http://www.giamusic.com

World Library Publications
3825 N. Willow Road
Schiller Park, IL 60176
1-800-566-6150
http://www.wlp.jspaluch.com

G. Schirmer
257 Park Ave South, 20th floor
New York, NY 10010
(212) 254-2100
http://www.schirmer.com

E.C. Schirmer
ECS Publishing
138 Ipswich Street
Boston, Massachusetts 02215-3534
(617) 236-1935
http://www.ecspublishing.com

Oxford University Press
Customer Service Department
2001 Evans Road
Cary, NC 27513
1-800-445-9714
http://www.oup-usa.org

Hinshaw Music, Inc.
PO Box 470
Chapel Hill, NC 27514
USA
1-800-568-7805
http://www.hinshawmusic.com/

Boosey and Hawkes
35 East 21st Street
New York
NY 10010-6212
(212) 358 5300
http://www.boosey.com/publishing/index.html

Belwin/Mills
15800 N.W. 48th Avenue
Miami, FL 33014
(305) 620-1500

We must make every effort to select texts that are scripturally based, that are theologically sound, and that support the church's teachings. "Feel-good" music and songs that are just "nice" are out! We need music that will support the rites and support the church (the people) that prays the rites. After you make a realistic assessment of what your choir can do, don't be afraid to mix styles at any given time. No musical diet can be one-sided and using a variety of musical styles will help keep things fresh and new.

Personnel

Chapter 24

There are many reasons why people come to the choir, and most of these are plausible. In general, whatever other reasons bring people to the choir, they offer their time and talents because of a love of music and a desire to serve God through the parish.

Start with what you have and rejoice in it! The people who make a commitment to the choir are your finest assets, and you as music director must tailor your plans with their unique capabilities in mind. If you only have a two- or three-part capability with your singers, for heaven's sake don't try to sing a chorus from "Messiah"! It will not only sound poorly, but will also discourage the singers you do have from becoming the best they can be. When music in liturgy is performed badly, it becomes a distraction and can cheapen the worship experience rather than enhance it. We want our choirs to take pride in their sound and in the work they do. Parishes today often employ section leaders (trained singers) to help volunteers learn more quickly and to provide a quartet as the nucleus of the choir. This can be very beneficial, but a word of caution is in order. If you are thinking of hiring a singer or singers, be absolutely clear about your specific expectations. A contract is best. For instance, does it include extra services above and beyond the weekly rehearsal and main Mass at which the choir sings?

One final issue dealing with personnel has to do with reading music. We as choir directors often assume that people who come to choir know the very basic elements of music reading; note values, rests, how to count, and the basic beat patterns of 2, 3, 4, and 6. This is often not the case. Once you have evaluated all of the voices in your choir (see the check-up in Chapter 3), if you find that many of them are not skilled in reading music stop trying to sing wonderful choral pieces and start laying a foundation for musicianship for your singers. My late organ teacher was so fond of saying, "I'd rather hear the wrong note at the right time, than all the right notes at the wrong time!" To choir directors, I say, "I'd rather hear the most humble, most simple piece, a unison hymn even, rendered beautifully than the finest piece of choral music done poorly!"

The goal in all of this is ministry to people. We need to take the wonderful gift that people can offer—their time and the gifts that God has given them—their voices and abilities and make the most of them. Anything less shows disrespect to the giver of all good gifts.

Recruiting New Choir Members

Chapter 25

In the previous chapter we gave thanks for the gifts of the voices you already have in your choir. This is the base upon which you will build. A well-organized and purposeful choir becomes, by its very nature, an important entity in any parish. In many places it is seen as a great source of pride because of the way it thrives and interacts with the assembly at worship. It is an involved, caring, praying group of people dedicated to the musical prayer life of the church. The old adage "nothing succeeds like success" is a theory we should all consider in the development of our choir organizations, especially if we expect to attract new members with any sort of regularity. Following is a list of some possible things you can do to recruit new members. First, ask yourself the question, "Why would anyone want to join our choir?" Put your responses on paper and translate them into a plan of action for recruiting.

1. Get the word out. Church members need to know who you are and what you do. Be visible personally at a variety of functions and invite people to join the choir.
2. Use your parish newsletter. Take advantage of this often-forgotten tool by writing regular columns about the choir and its activities. Always include an invitation to consider singing in the choir.
3. Have a Recruitment Sunday. Many parishes have fall and spring fairs where a large majority of the parish is present. Set up a booth for recruitment.
4. Coffee and Donuts. You and the choir attend and invite prospective members. You might

even sing something to get everyone's attention.

5. Newcomer receptions. Many parishes have evenings where those who have recently joined the parish are given an orientation to the parish and its ministers. Attend these and give a five-minute talk on music ministry and why singing in the choir is important. If your parish does not welcome the newcomers in this way, perhaps you should suggest starting this practice.
6. Publish a descriptive music ministry brochure. Have these available everywhere possible, and use signs and posters in creative ways.
7. Look for opportunities. There are lots of occasions in any parish to "push" the choir.

The point here is to make your program attractive to as many people as possible. A choir that sings well and prays well will have a special place in the life of the parish and people will want to consider joining. Very often all they need is just a little encouragement and a personal touch. Be involved and get others involved who can help you tailor a recruiting plan for your parish. Two heads are always better than one, and you can turn your ideas into a reality.

Maintenance of Choir Members

Chapter 26

There are many aspects of choir life that lend themselves to the keeping and maintenance of the choir itself. It is important for us as music directors to identify these aspects and use them as a source of ministry to our singers. It is a matter of both caring and respect.

1. Devise a yearly or twice yearly voice check for all members. This should be short (about five to seven minutes) to check range, reading skill, vowel production and breath control. It creates the personal touch and says, "I care about you and your voice."
2. Develop a descriptive brochure that spells out expectations and policies about such matters as attendance, rehearsal times and location, and other details. Keep in mind that it is important that these expectations mean something; for example, when someone misses more that two occasions in a row, call them to see if there is some health or other problem keeping them from attending rehearsals. Done in a caring way, this can let your choir members know that attendance at rehearsals is important while at the same time showing them you think they are important as well. There is a multitude of details you can include to reflect the needs of a specific choir situation. Tailor it to your needs and refer to it periodically when you think some aspect of your group's policies needs to be revisited.

3. Give your singers a monthly or bi-monthly calendar with all services and rehearsals listed, including extra things which always come up, and a short note of thanks and affirmation from you. Thanking your choir at every opportunity possible is very important. We want to keep them there and make sure they know we appreciate their time and efforts.
4. Pay special attention to birthdays, deaths, and other important personal events in the lives of your choir members. Keep records of when members have joined so that you can celebrate achievements of your choir members. Many of our members have been around for a long time—ten, 25, even 50 years. You might have an annual celebration for all those who have reached special milestones in your choir. A personal note to a new choir member after their first rehearsal, or to a singer who sings as a cantor or has a solo part for the first time, is a great way to boost morale. Occasionally a member of your choir will be part of other musical ensembles. Send a word of encouragement whenever your choir member has a major role in these productions. Keep a supply of cards for such occasions on hand, and let the other members of your choir sign them too. That kind of special touch counts.
5. Keep good records of such things ss telephone numbers, addresses (including e mail addresses), spouses' first names (always a hit!), and any other pertinent information you might need to have effective communication with your choir members. Everyone in the choir should receive an updated member roster/directory twice a year.

6. When choir members move to another city, their departure should include at least a prayer of blessing from you and your choir. You might also prepare a letter of introduction or a certificate of appreciation for the member to take to the choir director at their new parish.
7. While each choir is different, people who spend much time working together will often want to play together. There should at least be some form of annual appreciation for your singers (where you might acknowledge the milestones of various members) and some form of appreciation for the extra time that your choir gives over the paschal triduum.
8. Set short- and long-term goals with the choir and delegate certain responsibilities to other people. They generally want to help, and it will free you up to do other important things.

Choirs oftentimes become part of our extended families, and just as we do in our own personal families, we must take care to maintain those special relationships that make our lives rich and meaningful.

The Care and Feeding of a Choir Director

Chapter 27

The role of the choir director today is a double-edged sword; it's actually two big jobs rolled into one. Most of us know what it means to be a musician, but what does it mean to be a pastoral musician? Are these opposing terminologies? Some, I have heard say, simply are not pastoral because they fear that being so will somehow diminish their art. That may be so if art is your only concern. Granted, this can be a fine line to walk, but it is possible. The first order of business is to get our own egos under control. No matter how accomplished a musician you may be, you will always remain incompetent if you don't acquire those pastoral skills so necessary in the life of today's church. One of those important skills is learning to be a listener. Just as you must develop your ear for music, so must you develop your ear to hear what others are saying to you. Likewise, when we respond, we have to be good communicators.

We must learn to be present to the moment and cultivate a sense of love that overrides conflict; that is not easy. You see, the "pastoral" judgment must come first in our lives, because people are more important than something like perfection. If you cannot capture peoples' attention and imagination, you will never have the splendid opportunity to create any kind of musical/liturgical art anyway. The truth is that we can never be perfect, and the beauty of it all lies in that very imperfection, because there is only the one—Jesus Christ—who is perfect.

Today we have the unique opportunity and challenge of providing music which gives life to our rituals and draws all present into a closer union with our God and with each other.

Experience has taught us that while competent music expertise is essential, it remains but one component of the well-rounded pastoral musician. Today's parish demands that the music minister be a person of prayer, possessing a solid background in many areas if he or she is to truly effective in that role. As William Bauman has stated, if ministry is "service rendered out of love," our own ministry and how we minister has a powerful effect on our assemblies. This is why we work so hard to eliminate dissension and jealousy, to bury false pride and self-seeking, and to build a concern for worship as well as performance. Choir directors and church musicians should possess ability in a least the five following areas.

1. The art of communication. After all, this is what music is all about. An understanding of the power and potential of music is needed to enhance the word that is sung and heard, and to foster community.
2. The skill of performance. Technical proficiency in at least one area and sufficient familiarity to work intelligently in other areas is essential. i.e., how can the excellent organist lead and train choirs without a working knowledge of basic vocal technique?
3. A knowledge of repertoire. We should be familiar with not only the current trends, but also the classic repertoire of the past, because the old masters teach us about style, phrasing, and just about everything else. We need an extensive familiarity with hymns, chants, folk songs, various settings of important texts, and contemporary compositions.
4. A knowledge of basic liturgical principles and the scriptures. Musicians must be proclaimers of the word, too. And, we must know the lectionary years, A, B and C in order to tell the stories of those cycles through song. We must

also have a working knowledge of the rites of the church, not just the order of Mass.

5. An ability to utilize interpersonal, organizational, and managerial skills is a must.

This may seem like too much to expect of one person, and granted, there are many facets to consider. However, to "minister" well, one must be extremely well-equipped for that specific ministry. Many of you may be thinking, "… but I don't have time for school, what with family and job pressures," and that may be the case. There are other alternatives to learn besides formal study; it is never too late, and we are never too old to start. Some effective alternatives to formal education might include:

1. Private lessons—not just piano, organ, or voice, but perhaps music theory and conducting.
2. Singing in a good choir—especially in a civic chorus where performance is stressed. You can learn a great deal by observing what others do.
3. Summer courses—one- to six-week seminars are widely available in a variety of locations and the short term is usually easy to manage.
4. Read and study everything possible that is pertinent to the field so that you can develop a sense of the fitness of things.

There is no other way to become excellent, or even good, at our craft without spending the time necessary to hone that craft. For choir directors, it means excellence in many areas, and it takes many years of very hard work to bring this kind of artistry to maturity.

This brings up a core issue: should you be a choir director? If we take seriously the important ministries to which a choir director must attend, we must acknowledge honestly that not everyone is cut out to be a choir director. If you are feeling overwhelmed by the size of the task, that is normal, especially for a new director; however, if after a lot of prayer and reflection you honestly do not believe that you want to do several of the tasks called for in these pages, you might have to think about not taking on the role of the director. If the musical aspect appeals to you but the administrative part does not, consider recruiting a manager for the choir. If the musical aspects are well beyond your abilities, perhaps you are the one who could offer to manage all the other aspects of having a choir, or perhaps you are the one to be the librarian or social coordinator for a choir. There are many tasks and a choir director can divide them among several people. At the end of the day, however, there needs to be a director—the one who embodies the choir and leads it to ever more prayerful, joy-filled and excellent service to the church through the art of choral singing.

These are indeed exciting times for us as choir directors and pastoral musicians, and today's church calls us to minister with a deft hand. We must live in the tension of music as art and music as ministry—they DO go hand in hand. Music in worship must be true art and true prayer. We all recognize the artistry of J.S. Bach, especially when we hear his monumental "St. Matthew Passion," or perhaps the "Mass in B Minor," but can you imagine what old Bach must have understood about prayer to have written such pieces?

Other Issues and a Final Word

Chapter 28

There are a couple of other issues that need to be addressed as we draw our time together to a close. One is the relationship you have with the pastor, especially in terms of budgeting for the music program, and to deal with ways of keeping your interest in choral singing alive and well.

Contracts

Should you have a contract with the pastor, even if you are a volunteer? Probably. In our ministry there are just too many variables and opportunities for misunderstanding. The associations of musicians and choir directors (see the next paragraph) all have guidelines for what needs to be in a contract, including salary scales, evaluation processes and the like. A contract is just a good idea to avoid possible conflicts with the pastor and the parish. It will also help you in terms of knowing what power you have. There may be people who should not be members of your choir for any number of reasons. You need to know if you have the right to ask people not join your choir. Do you have the authority to hire other musicians, section leaders and the like? How does the parish deal with complaints? You would be well advised to keep a file of all the letters of praise and the signed letters of complaint that come to you or the pastor. I make it a point to not give any weight to anonymous letters or to verbal compliments or complaints, but again, does the pastoral staff concur with this policy? Clarity in all of these things will make your relationship with the pastoral staff and the pastor much smoother, and should lead to a much stronger place for the parish music program in the parish structure.

Budgets

Even if you are a volunteer conductor of a six-voice choir, you need to have a budget. Monies are needed for purchasing new music, for hiring that trumpet player twice a year and for your memberships in various associations. Asking for money on a case-by-case basis is generally very time-consuming for both you and the pastor: If the pastoral team is willing, it is much better to ask for money once through the use of an annual budget. If you are directing a large choir in a parish of some means, a budget is certainly expected. Following is a copy of the budget categories that I have used for several years. The amounts will vary across the country, but the needs are fairly universal. I have included several of the expenses that will only be used if you are also responsible for the parish liturgy budget. Feel free to use some or all of these as you prepare to ask for the money you need for the coming year.

General Budget Categories

Salaries – Full or Part Time
Stipends
- Cantors
- Section Leaders
- Instrumentalists
- Substitute Organists

Materials
- Training
- Education
  - Cantors
  - Other Ministries (Lectors, Eucharistic Ministers if in your area)
- Music Repertoire
  - Children's Choir
  - Adult Choir
  - Instrumental Parts and Keyboard Music
  - Hymnal Replacement

Art and Environment
- Worship Programs
- Seasonal Decorations
  - Flowers

Administration
- Publicity
- Reprint Licenses
- Computer Software, Maintenance and Equipment
- Office Supplies
- Postage

Instrument Maintenance and Tuning
- Pianos
- Organs
- Other Instruments

Continuing Education
- Director
- Other Ministers
- Travel Expenses

Hospitality
- In-service Expenses
- Weekly Rehearsal Refreshments

Organizations

Keeping your interest in directing choir alive is not always a simple matter. If nothing else, reading the past twenty-five chapters should have made you aware of the amount of time and effort a choir can consume. One way of keeping your spirits up on an ongoing basis is to join one or more of the associations that support people like us. Following is a list of these organizations and their addresses.

American Guild of Organists (AGO)
475 Riverside Drive, Suite 1260
New York, NY 10115
(212) 870-2310
http://www.agohq.org

American Choral Directors Associations (ACDA)
502 SW 38th Street
Lawton Oklahoma 73505
(580) 355-8161
http://acdaonline.org/

National Association of Pastoral Musicians (NPM)
225 Sheridan Street, NW
Washington, DC 20011-1492
Phone (202) 723-5800
http://www.npm.org/

Choristers' Guild
2834 W. Kingsley Rd.
Garland, TX 75041-2498
972-271-1521
http://www.choristersguild.org/

Diocesan and other choirs

Finally, choir directors can get a lot of solace by joining a larger choir. Many dioceses have a massed choir that sings for diocesan events such as the Chrism Mass. Some have extensive rehearsal schedules while others rely more on the abilities of the singers who participate than on rehearsals. Or look to joining a choir that sings for civic events. Singing with others can often remind you of why you do this in the first place.

Conclusion

I know that many of you get very excited about music ministry when you attend a convention or other inspiring workshop, and I urge you to hold on to those feelings for as long as possible. However, put those feelings into action. Perhaps the first thing to do is to take an inventory of your current strengths and weaknesses, and start creating some plans for your success. Here are some suggestions you might consider as you are mapping your strategy:

- Get the training you need. A little talent and lots of good will may not be enough.
- Set realistic goals for yourself and for the choir. Take little steps!
- Rely on the help of others, especially in your weaker areas.
- Cultivate a sense of artistry in your life.
- Deepen your own personal prayer life.

In developing your plans, remember that they are not written down anywhere in a book—they are in your mind and in your heart. Also, remember that while we are called to live competently and confidently, our work IS about communication, that essential quality which brings any music to life. We are called to communicate our faith in Jesus Christ, and that faith, lived in our diverse cultures, demands of us an inter-disciplinary vision that weaves together, like the basket weaver, the harmonies of the past with the life themes of today. Howard Swann, in his writings on choral music, has said it best and I join my voice with his to urge you to "have *faith*—faith in our God, and in yourselves, and in one another; have *hope*—hope that those who hear us and join in our music-making will understand what our music is saying; and have *love*—which by musical means, combines beauty and art, form and sound, the personal and the objective, release and fulfillment, appreciation and understanding; love—working through the power of music to transform lives for an hour, a year, or a lifetime."

Ten Commandments for Choir Directors

1. *Be prepared – Plan your work and know your music; use your time effectively.*

2. *Be goal oriented – Plan at least six months ahead.*

3. *Be present to your community – Minister according to the local customs of your parish.*

4. *Be caring – People entrust themselves to you, both spiritually AND vocally*

5. *Be prayerful – Deepen your own prayer life.*

6. *Be positive, sensitive and of good character – Acquire good interpersonal skills in management and conflict-solving.*

7. *Be knowledgeable – Know the lectionary, the liturgy and the rites of the Church. Familiarize yourself with ALL musical styles.*

8. *Be conscientious – Improve your vocal, choral and conducting techniques.*

9. *Be current – Read choral and liturgical journals. Read and re-read* ***Music in Catholic Worship***

10. *Be open to beauty – Cultivate a sense of artistry in your life.*

Oliver Douberly

Selected Bibliography

Part ONE: Music

Alderson, Richard. *Complete Handbook of Voice Training.* New York: Parker Publishing Co., Inc., 1979.

Apel, Willi, ed. *Harvard Dictionary of Music.* 2nd edition revised and enlarged. Cambridge, MA: Harvard University Press, 1969.

Baker, Theodore, ed. *Pronouncing Pocket-Manual of Musical Terms, revised edition.* New York: G. Schirmer, Inc., 1947.

Dart, Thurston. *The Interpretation of Music,* Harper Calophon Books. New York: Harper and Row, 1963.

Decker, Harold A. and Herford, Julius, eds. *Choral Conducting: A Symposium, 2nd edition.* Englewood Cliffs, NJ: Prentice Hall, Inc., 1988.

Ehmann, Wilhelm. *Choral Directing.* Minneapolis, MN: Augsburg Press, 1968.

Fellerer, Karl Gustav. *The History of Catholic Church Music.* Baltimore: Helicon Press, 1961.

Funk, Virgil C., ed. *Music in Catholic Worship: The NPM Commentary, revised edition.* Washington, DC: Pastoral Press, 1984.

Garretson, Robert L. *Conducting Choral Music, 7th edition.* Englewood Cliffs, NJ: Prentice Hall, 1993.

Huijbers, Bernard. *The Performing Audience, 2nd edition.* Phoenix, AZ: North American Liturgical Resources, 1980.

Marhsall, Madeleine. *The Singer's Manual of English Diction.* New York: G. Schirmer, 1953.

McElheran, Brock. *Conducting Techniques for Beginners and Professionals.* New York: Oxford University Press, 1966.

Moe, Daniel. *Basic Choral Concepts.* Minneapolis, MN: Augsburg Press, 1972.

Moe, Daniel. *Problems in Conducting.* Minneaplis, MN: Augsburg Press, 1968.

Pfoutsch, Lloyd. *English Diction for the Singer* New York: Lawson Gould – G. Schirmer, 1971.

Routeley, Erik. *The Church and Music.* London: Gerald Duckworth, 1967.

Trusler, Ivan. *The Choral Director's Latin.* Lanham, MD: University Press of America, 1987.

Ulrich, Homer. *A Survey of Choral Music.* New York: Harcourt Brace Jovanovich, Inc., 1973.

Part TWO: Liturgy

Hoffman, Elizabeth, ed. *The Liturgy Documents: A Parish Resource.* 3rd Edition. Chicago: Liturgy Training Publications, 1991

Lysik, David A., ed. *The Liturgy Documents: A Parish Resource,* Volume 2. Chicago: Liturgy Training Publications, 2000.

Huck, Gabe. *Liturgy with Style and Grace.* Chicago: Liturgy Training Publications. 1984.

Rendler, Elaine. *In the Midst of the Assembly.* Portland, OR: Pastoral Press, 1994.

The Music Documents: Music in Catholic Worship and Liturgical Music Today. Portland, OR: Pastoral Press, 1995.

Rendler, Elaine. *This is the Day*. Portland, OR: Pastoral Press 1995.

Saliers, Don E. *Worship and Spirituality.* Philadelphia: The Westminster Presss, 1984.

Johnson, Lawrence J. *The Word & Eucharist Handbook.* San Jose: Resource Publications, 1986.

Fleming, Austin & Tufano, Victoria. *Preparing for Liturgy: A Theology and Spirituality, revised edition* Chicago: Liturgy Training Publications, 1977.

Searle, Mark. *Liturgy Made Simple.* Collegeville, MN: Liturgical Press, 1981.

Kavanagh, Aidan. *Elements of Rite: A Handbook of Liturgical Style*. New York: Pueblo Publishing Co., 1982.

Johnson, Lawrence J. *The Mystery of Faith: the Ministers of Music.* Portland, OR: Pastoral Press. 1983.

Other Titles in the BASICS Series:

Cantor, Revised Edition
James Hansen, Melanie Coddigton, Joe Simons

Children's Choir
David Nastal

Classroom Prayer
Vivian Williams

Infant Baptism: A Parish Program
Christopher Heller

Parish Liturgy
William Belford